The Resilient Black Woman: Stories of Faith, Hope, and Resilience

A 31 Day Devotional

Dr. Natasha Booker, LCSW

Copyright © 2025 Dr. Natasha Booker All rights reserved

The characters and events portrayed in this book are fictitious. Any similarity to real persons, living or dead, is coincidental and not intended by the author.

No part of this book may be reproduced, or stored in a retrieval system, or transmitted in any form or by any means, electronic, mechanical, photocopying, recording, or otherwise, without express written permission of the publisher.

Scripture quotations taken from the Holy Bible, New International Version®, NIV®. Copyright © 1973, 1978, 1984, 2011 by Biblica, Inc.® Used by permission. All rights reserved worldwide.

For further information about the NIV, visit www.biblica.com.First Edition:

April 2025 ISBN: 979-8-218-66719-1Published by Dr. Natasha Booker Printed in the United States of America.

This book is dedicated to Black women everywhere! May you be seen, heard, and loved!

Acknowledgments

To my husband, Dion, I love loving you! Thank you for always believing in me. To my children (Lexi, Deja, Mondre', and Courtney), you rock! We are not created to journey through life alone. If we are fortunate enough, we collect priceless treasures called friends that journey with us. To all my friends who have traveled with me, thank you for your love and support. To my one and only mother, Rev. Nancy Kingwood-Small, your love, support, and discipline have made me the woman I am today. Thank you! To my prayer partners, your prayers have carried me through some of my darkest moments. You are my angels. And shoutout to God, who makes all things possible!

Introduction

In life's journey, we, as Black women, often find ourselves navigating a landscape filled with beauty and burden. Our experiences are woven with the rich tapestry of our culture, history, and faith—a faith that has been the bedrock of our resilience for generations. We stand on the shoulders of those who came before us: women who persevered through unspeakable trials yet emerged with a song of victory. This book, The Resilient Black Woman, is a testament to that enduring spirit, written for every sister who has ever felt the world's weight on her shoulders yet continues to rise with the dawn.

As a Black woman and a follower of Christ, I know firsthand the unique challenges that come with our identity. We face the daily trials of systemic injustice, the pain of generational trauma, and the personal battles that life inevitably brings. Yet, within us lies a profound strength—one that is both deeply personal and undeniably collective. Our faith in God, coupled with the richness of our culture, forms a robust foundation that sustains us through the darkest valleys and propels us toward the mountaintops of triumph.

The Resilient Black Woman is more than a collection of stories, prayers, and affirmations. It is a celebration of our journey—a journey marked by struggle but also by immense victory. Through the lens of faith, we will explore how God's promises intersect with our lived experiences as Black women. We will delve into the Scriptures that have comforted us, the prayers that have lifted us, and the affirmations that have empowered us to keep moving forward, even when the road seemed impossible.

This book is for you, my sister. Whether it's in the midst of a storm or standing on the other side, I hope you will find the encouragement and inspiration to press on within these pages. I want you to see that you are not alone—your struggles are understood, your pain is valid, and your victories are celebrated. Together, we will reflect on how God has brought us through and how our faith, intertwined with our culture, has enabled us to overcome.

Let us embark on this journey together, hand in hand, heart to heart, knowing that with God on our side, we are more than conquerors. May this book be a source of strength, hope, and empowerment as you continue to walk in the fullness of who God created you to be—a beautiful, resilient, victorious Black woman of faith.

This devotional will focus on:

1. **Building spiritual resilience**: Drawing strength from God to endure and grow through difficulties.
2. **Overcoming generational and societal challenges**: Acknowledging the unique struggles Black women face, such as systemic racism, generational trauma, and the Strong Black Woman stereotype, while affirming their worth and purpose in God.
3. **Celebrating victories—big and small**: Encouraging women to recognize triumphs in their lives as evidence of God's faithfulness.
4. **Living victoriously**: Empowering women to walk in their God-given identity, no longer defined by their struggles but by their faith and God's promises.

The layout for each day is a scripture of meditation, a story, prayer, affirmation, and reflection questions. Take your time! Spend 30 minutes a day with this daily devotional. Find the comfort you need for each day.

Are you ready? Let's go!

Prologue

Life has a way of throwing curveballs. Life, at times, doesn't fight fair. Everything can be great one day, and your life is turned upside down the next. What do you do? Where do you turn? How do you make it through? These are answers I have asked myself repeatedly. I do not have a blanket answer to any of these questions. I only know what got me through. It was prayer, affirmation, and community with other Black women. I started this devotional by sharing my story: one of tragedy, hope, and resilience.

Lord Help!! Why have thou forsaken me?

It was March 26, 2002, I was 35 weeks pregnant when sharp pains shot through my stomach and lower back. It was 5 AM, what is happening? Am I going into early labor? I thought. The contractions were intense. I was rushed to the hospital where I was checked and rechecked. The contractions intensified, and the pain was unbearable, but I was not in labor. The nurse gave me medication to stop the contractions. The on-duty doctors and nurses continued to check me. It was just my son's father and I in the room while I was hooked up to a lot of machines. More doctors came in and there was a lot of chatter, more checking, and tests.

Finally, my doctor arrived. I was checked and rechecked-more tests, more sonograms. Still, no one was able to tell me what was going on. The contractions had stopped due to the medication. I was at ease. My doctor finally told me that my son no longer had a heartbeat. He continued to say my son had died, and now I had to be prepped for delivery. He said it so fast; I could not comprehend what he said. I was in shock and was speechless for a few minutes. After a brief period, I was finally able to speak, but nothing came out, just a devastated and bewildered cry. I was filled with emotions.

I recall my following statement being, "I still have to give birth?" I was still in shock. My doctor looked at me with sympathetic eyes and said, "Yes." More tears. More overwhelming emotions. The first call I made was to my mother. I told her the news, and she began to cry. She asked questions that I could not answer. I had no answers. All I knew was that my son had died. I didn't believe it. I was in denial.

My son's father immediately began to console me, while tears ran down his face and soaked my forehead. We both cried because there was nothing, we could say to each other. Finally, being able to gather my thoughts, I asked, "What happened?" No one could answer me. All they knew was that my son didn't have a heartbeat and that I was bleeding internally. So much, so fast. Still, no answers.

The doctors and nurses began to prep me for delivery. The medication the nurse gave me earlier stopped my contractions, and now they had to restart them. For 24 hours, I was given pill after pill; my body would not go into labor. I was bleeding internally, and my uterus would not contract. After 24 hours of trying to induce labor, my doctor told me I would need a cesarean because I was losing a lot of blood. I was emotionally numb. He also told me that if he could not stop the bleeding, he would have to perform a hysterectomy. However, before he could perform the cesarean, he needed my permission for the hysterectomy because he did not know what he would find once the surgery started. I was once again speechless and I thought to myself, a hysterectomy!! I am only 22 years old. This can't be!! I was in no shape to make such a life-changing decision. I had a 2-year-old already, but I was unsure if I wanted more children later in life. However, I did not have a choice but to sign the forms. My life was on the line. My fate was in God's hands. I was in bad shape.

My mother, who always believed in prayer, called our Pastor and other clergy to pray with me. In no time, I was prepped and taken to the operating room. What happened from there was out of my control. When I woke up, I was in a recovery room, a little groggy, still confused, and in physical and emotional pain.

I vaguely remember my doctor saying he did not need to perform a hysterectomy. He was able to stop the bleeding. He then inquired if I wanted to see my son for a few minutes. Mekhi weighed five pounds and seven ounces. He had grey eyes and a head full of hair. All his fingers and toes were accounted for. He was beautiful. He looked like he was asleep. He was resting peacefully with the angels.

My doctor was finally able to explain what caused me to have a stillborn. Somehow, the umbilical cord wrapped around my son's neck. I also had blood clots in my uterus that caused internal bleeding. My doctor could not explain WHY it happened outside of the physical and scientific explanation. I had a healthy pregnancy. I took my vitamins and ate as I was supposed to.

Over the next few days, I had around-the-clock visitors and phone calls; however, I was not out of the woods. I had lost so much blood that I needed a blood transfusion. Well, not just a blood transfusion; I had ten of them. The blood transfusions caused an allergic reaction. My heart started racing. I was given Benadryl and some other medications to help stabilize my heart. My next stop was the intensive care unit. I was still numb from losing my son, and now I had to deal with my own health issues. Before this ordeal, I had always been healthy. Finally, my heart rate returned to normal, and my hemoglobin increased.

I was discharged from the hospital after six days, just in time to bury my son. I had to say goodbye to my son, who never took a breath. I dreaded the upcoming days. My mom and sisters made the funeral arrangements. I just had to show up, and I didn't even want to do that. It was a graveside funeral. Very quick, less than 20 minutes. It's just the way I requested it. Surrounded by my loved ones and friends. I said goodbye to Mekhi. I recall the day as if it was yesterday. My mother was strong and pushed through the planning, but the actual funeral was too much for her. She was overwhelmed. She collapsed at the funeral. It was too much for all of us to bear.

In the coming days, everyone returned to work and resumed their everyday lives. I thought to myself, how do I go on? How do I pick up the pieces? I don't know why a piece of me had been stolen. Why did God do this to me? Why did God even allow me to get pregnant just to take my son? Why?? Why??? Why?? What did I do wrong? Why did my body fail me? WHY?

I put on a façade when visitors came to the house, but I cried all night. My heart was broken. I didn't understand, and I was mad at God. Days and weeks went by. I was consumed with grief. I didn't have the strength to care for my son, Mondre. I didn't want to go anywhere or see anyone. As time went on, I had to re-emerge back into life. I started by going to church. On my first Sunday back, someone asked me where my baby was? Tears streamed down my face as I told them he died. The questions re-ignited anger and uncontrollable grief. I had a cesarean scare but no baby to show for it. All I could do was cry and pray!

Thank God the story did not end there. With much prayer and support, I started my healing journey. Today, I still don't know why I went through this BUT what I can say is that God has restored my joy. I don't know what the future holds, I just know that God is in control, and I can do hard things!

You see, this book isn't just for you; it's for me, too! So, Sis, come with me. Let's walk this path together. Let's talk about how we keep our faith strong and navigate this life with grace, dignity, and a whole lot of Black girl magic. It's time to tell our story, lift each other, and show the world just who we are!

DAY 1

Scripture: Isaiah 43:1-2

But now, this is what the LORD says— he who created you, Jacob, he who formed you, Israel: "Do not fear, for I have redeemed you; I have summoned you by name; you are mine. When you pass through the waters, I will be with you, and when you pass through the rivers, they will not sweep over you. When you walk through the fire, you will not be burned; the flames will not set you ablaze.

Devotional:

Delia stood at the empty crossroads, staring down the dusty roads stretching before her. Her heartbeat was so loud it felt like echoing in the still air. Everything behind her? A trainwreck. Her house? Gone—foreclosed last month. Her job? Cutbacks. And her marriage? That fell apart long before the other pieces of her life started crumbling.

Now, here she was, standing at this literal and figurative crossroads. Each path promised something different, but none came with a guarantee. A new life was out there somewhere, but figuring out which way to go felt impossible.

She kicked at a rock near her sneaker, the weight of everything pressing down on her. For a second, she thought about just sitting in the dirt and calling it quits. But then, like a voice cutting through the fog in her brain, she heard her grandmother's words—the ones she'd heard a million times growing up. The image of her grandma came back so vividly it almost made Delia smile: sitting in her favorite chair, Bible open on her lap, her voice steady and full of conviction:

"Do not fear, for I have redeemed you.

I have summoned you by name; you are mine."

Delia took a long breath, her chest feeling a little less tight. Grandma always knew how to make her feel like she could do hard things, even when the world felt stacked against her.

She thought about the women in her family who had stood at their crossroads, unsure of what lay ahead but moving forward anyway. Her great grandma left everything behind during the Great Migration and headed north with nothing but faith. Her mom entered her first corporate job as the only Black woman in the office and proved she belonged there. And all the aunties and church ladies who sang their way through struggles, lifting themselves and everyone around them.

Delia took a deep breath, and as if on cue, another verse her grandma used to love filled her mind:

"When you walk through the fire,

you will not be burned; the flames will not set you ablaze."
(Isaiah 43:2 NIV)

She glanced down each road again. They still looked long and uncertain, but something shifted inside her. She wasn't doing this alone. She had never been. The same God who carried her ancestors through slavery, through Jim Crow, through every challenge they'd faced—He was still with her, walking beside her.

"Alright," Delia muttered to herself, straightening up a little. "Let's do this."

She picked a direction—maybe the left road, the right, it didn't matter—and started walking. Her sneakers kicked up dust with every step, and her legs felt shaky at first, but she kept moving. Then, without even thinking, she started humming. It was low at first, almost under her breath, but the words came back to her like they were stitched into her soul:

"Wade in the water, wade in the water, children, wade in the water, God's a-going to trouble the water."

Her grandmother had taught her that song years ago, and singing it now felt like a lifeline. She thought about all the women who had stood at their crossroads, choosing to keep moving even when the road ahead was uncertain. Their strength was her strength. Their grit was her grit.

As she kept walking, her steps got a little lighter. The fear that had been sitting heavy on her chest started to melt away. She didn't know exactly what was waiting for her down this road, but she didn't feel stuck for the first time in a long time. She felt... free.

When she reached a hill and looked back at the crossroads behind her, Delia felt tears sting her eyes. She'd made a choice. She'd taken the first step. And that was no small thing.

She took a deep breath, raised her face to the sky, and said, "Thank you." It wasn't loud or dramatic. It was just honest. She wasn't where she wanted to be but was on her way. And for the first time in what felt like forever, that was enough.

Prayer:

God, thank you for the assurance that you are always with us, even in our darkest moments. Help us to remember that we are yours and that you will guide us through every trial. Strengthen our faith and fill us with your peace. In Jesus' name, Amen.

Affirmation:

I am fearfully and wonderfully made, called by name, and never alone. God's presence strengthens me through every challenge.

Reflection Questions:

- Isaiah 43:1 says, *"Fear not, for I have redeemed you; I have called you by name, you are mine."* How does knowing that God has redeemed and called you by name empower you daily as a Black woman? In what ways can this assurance help you overcome fear and anxiety?
- *"When you pass through the waters, I will be with you; and through the rivers, they shall not overwhelm you."* Reflect on a time when you faced overwhelming challenges. How did God's presence sustain you during that time? How can you apply this promise to current situations in your life?
- The verse speaks about walking "through fire" and not being burned. What "fires" have you faced or are currently facing as a Black woman, whether in your personal life, career, or community? How does this scripture reassure you of God's protection and guidance through those trials?
- Isaiah 43:2 highlights God's promise of protection during difficult times. How can this passage inspire you to support and uplift other Black women in your community? What practical steps can you take to be a source of strength and encouragement to those around you?

Notes:

DAY 2

Scripture: Matthew 17:20

"He replied, "Because you have so little faith. Truly, I tell you, if you have faith as small as a mustard seed, you can say to this mountain, 'Move from here to there,' and it will move. Nothing will be impossible for you."

Devotional:

Ava stared at the mountain before her, its imposing presence casting a shadow over everything she'd worked for. This mountain wasn't made of rock and earth but systemic barriers, generational trauma, and societal expectations that seemed impossible to overcome.

She clutched the small pendant around her neck – a tiny glass sphere containing a single mustard seed. It had been passed down through generations of women in her family, a tangible reminder of their faith and resilience.

As Ava stood there, doubt creeping into her heart, she heard the gentle voices of the women who came before her, whispering the words that had sustained them: "Truly, I tell you, if you have faith as small as a mustard seed, you can say to this mountain, 'Move from here to there,' and it will move. Nothing will be impossible for you."

Ava closed her eyes, remembering the stories of her ancestors: her great-great-grandmother, who'd taught herself to read by candlelight after long days in the fields; her grandmother, who'd marched for civil rights and faced water hoses and police dogs with unwavering courage; and her mother, who'd become the first in their family to graduate college while raising three children on her own. Each of these women had faced their mountains. Each had held onto faith no bigger than a mustard seed, yet that faith had moved mountains.

Taking a deep breath, Ava opened her eyes and looked at the mountain before her. She was the first Black woman to be considered for partnership at her law firm, but the old boys' network seemed impenetrable. The weight of representation sat heavily on her shoulders – she knew her success or failure would impact opportunities for other Black women coming after her. "Lord," Ava whispered, "my faith might be small, but it's all I've got. Help me move this mountain."

With renewed determination, Ava strode forward. She pored over case files late into the night, mentored young Black girls interested in law, and spoke up in meetings even when her voice shook. Slowly but surely, she saw shifts in the firm's culture. Months passed. The day of the partnership decision arrived. As Ava sat in the boardroom, surrounded by faces that looked nothing like hers, she felt the weight of that mustard seed against her chest. Tears sprang to Ava's eyes when the senior partner announced her name. The mountain hadn't disappeared overnight, but it had moved. A path had been cleared for her and others to follow.

That evening, Ava celebrated with her mother, aunts, and cousins. As they shared stories and laughter, Ava realized that her victory wasn't hers alone. It belonged to all the Black women who'd held onto faith in the face of impossible odds. Her aunt Beatrice, eyes glistening with pride, took Ava's hand. "Baby girl, do you remember what your grandma used to say?" Ava nodded, her voice joining with the other women as they recited together:

"Faith of a mustard seed might seem small, but it's enough to make mountains fall.

Black woman, stand tall, let your light shine through, for with God, there's nothing you can't do."

As Ava looked around at the firm, beautiful Black women surrounding her, she understood more deeply than ever the power of faith passed down through generations. Her mustard seed had moved a mountain, and she knew their faith could reshape the world.

Prayer:

"Lord, help me to have faith that can move mountains, even when the world tries to weigh me down. Strengthen my belief in the power You've placed within me and let that faith shine through every challenge I face."

Affirmation:

I am powerful in my faith, and with it, I can overcome any obstacle that stands in my way.

Reflection Questions:

- What does faith mean to you daily as a Black woman?
- Can you share a time when your faith helped you overcome a significant challenge?
- How can you cultivate mustard seed-sized faith in the face of societal pressures and personal hardships?

Notes:

DAY 3

Scripture: Isaiah 41:10

"So do not fear, for I am with you; do not be dismayed, for I am your God. I will strengthen and help you and uphold you with my righteous right hand."

Devotional:

Imani stood before the mirror, her hands trembling as she adjusted her suit jacket. Today was the day she'd worked towards for years - her first argument before the Supreme Court. As a Black woman and civil rights attorney, she carried not just her dreams but the hopes of her community on her shoulders.

The weight of it all threatened to crush her. Doubt crept in, whispering that she wasn't good enough and didn't belong in those hallowed halls of justice.

Just then, her phone buzzed. It was a text from her mother: "Remember Isaiah 41:10, baby girl. You've got this." Imani closed her eyes and recited the verse she'd known since childhood:

"So do not fear, for I am with you; do not be dismayed, for I am your God.

I will strengthen you and help you; I will uphold you with my righteous right hand."

As she spoke the words, Imani felt a warmth spread through her body. She opened her eyes and gazed at her reflection, seeing herself for the first time that morning. In her dark skin, she saw the strength of her ancestors who had survived the Middle Passage. She saw the crown of her heritage, a legacy of beauty and resilience in her tightly coiled hair. In her eyes, she saw the fire of generations of Black women who had fought for justice and equality.

"I am with you," the verse had said, and Imani realized it wasn't just God speaking those words. It was her grandmother who cleaned houses to put her children through school. It was her mother, who had been the first in their family to go to college. Every Black woman had paved the way for her to stand where she is today.

Imani straightened her back and lifted her chin. "I will strengthen you and help you," she repeated, feeling the power of those words course through her veins. She was not alone in this fight. She carried the strength of her faith and the indomitable spirit of Black womanhood.

As she picked up her briefcase and headed for the door, Imani paused for one last look in the mirror. Gone was the trembling, uncertain woman of moments ago. In her place stood a warrior, upheld by the righteous right hand of God and the unbreakable sisterhood of Black women throughout history.

"Let's go make some history," Imani said to her reflection, a determined smile on her face.

She entered the world ready to argue her case and the cause of justice itself. With each click of her heels on the pavement, Imani felt the rhythm of her ancestors' heartbeats urging her forward. Fear had no place here, and dismay was left behind.

For she was strengthened, helped, and upheld, and in that strength, Imani knew she would prevail.

Prayer:

God, I thank You for being my constant support and strength. When I feel alone, remind me that You are always with me. Let Your presence be a source of courage and peace as I walk through life's challenges.

Affirmation:

I am never alone; God's presence surrounds me, and God's strength upholds me.

Reflection Questions:

- What fears do you face, and how does this scripture help you confront them?
- In what ways have you felt God's presence and support in your life?
- How can this scripture empower you to support other Black women in your community?
- Reflect on the affirmation "I am not alone; God is with me" and share a personal story that illustrates this truth.

Notes:

DAY 4

Scripture: Philippians 4:13

"I can do all this through him, who gives me strength."

Devotional:

Aisha's lungs burned as she pushed herself up the steep hill. This was mile 20 of the marathon, where many runners hit the wall. But for Aisha, this race was about more than just crossing a finish line. It was about proving to herself - and the world - that she could overcome any obstacle.

As her legs threatened to give out, Aisha's mind flashed back to where her journey began. She saw herself as a young girl in a rundown neighborhood, watching her single mother work multiple jobs to keep food on the table. She remembered the teachers who told her she'd never amount to much, the doors that seemed to close in her face at every turn. But then she heard her grandmother's voice, strong and clear as it had been all those years ago: "Baby girl, remember Philippians 4:13 - 'I can do all things through Christ who strengthens me.'"

Those words had been her lifeline through the most challenging times: when she struggled to pay for college, working nights and studying days; when she faced discrimination in her corporate job, being passed over for promotions despite her qualifications; when she decided to leave that world behind and start her own business, facing skepticism and setbacks at every turn.

As she pushed her body to its limits in this marathon, Aisha realized that each struggle had prepared her for this moment. Every setback had made her stronger, and every obstacle had taught her resilience. "I can do all things," she whispered through gritted teeth as she crested the hill. The words gave her a second wind, and she picked up her pace.

As she ran, Aisha thought about all the Black women who had run their marathons before her—women like Harriet Tubman, who had guided enslaved people to freedom, Mary McLeod Bethune, who fought for education and civil rights, and Mae Jemison, who had reached for the stars and made it to space.

These women hadn't just survived—they had triumphed. They had done so not just through their strength, but through the power of their faith and the support of their communities.

Aisha's feet pounded the pavement, each step a declaration of her strength and the collective power of Black womanhood. She was running not just for herself but for every Black girl who had been told she couldn't, shouldn't, or would fail.

As the finish line came into view, Aisha felt a surge of energy. The crowd cheered, but in her mind, she heard the voices of her ancestors urging her on. She heard her grandmother's prayers, her mother's encouragement, and her sisters' laughter in struggle and triumph.

With a final burst of speed, Aisha crossed the finish line, her arms raised in victory. Tears streamed down her face as the reality of her achievement sank in. She had done it. She had run her race, kept the faith, and triumphed.

As the medal was placed around her neck, Aisha knew this was more than a personal victory. It was a testament to the strength within every Black woman—the strength to overcome, persevere, and triumph against all odds.

"I can do all things through Christ who strengthens me," Aisha whispered, touching the medal. And in that moment, she knew that this was just the beginning. There were more races to run, mountains to climb, and victories to claim.

But now she knew, without a doubt, that she had the strength to face whatever lay ahead, for she was a Black woman, strengthened by faith, empowered by heritage, unstoppable in her determination to rise, overcome, and triumph.

Prayer:

Lord, empower me to accomplish all that You have set before me. When I doubt my abilities, remind me that I have the strength to do all things through You. Guide me as I work towards my goals and dreams.

Affirmation:

I am capable and strong, and through Christ, I can achieve anything I set my mind to.

Reflection Questions:

- How do you draw strength from Christ in your everyday activities and responsibilities?
- Describe a situation where you felt empowered by this verse to accomplish something difficult.
- How can this scripture inspire you to uplift and support other Black women?
- What does the affirmation "I am capable of achieving greatness" mean to you, and how can you apply it?

Notes:

DAY 5

Scripture: 2 Corinthians 5:7

"For we live by faith, not by sight."

Devotional:

Tanya stared at the pregnancy test in her trembling hands, the two pink lines blurring as tears filled her eyes. At 35, she had finally mustered the courage to leave her abusive husband, and now this. Single, jobless, and pregnant - it felt like the universe was playing a cruel joke on her.

As panic threatened to overwhelm her, a quiet voice in her heart whispered the words her late mother used to say: "For we walk by faith, not by sight." 2 Corinthians 5:7.

Tanya closed her eyes, letting the familiar verse wash over her. She thought about the generations of Black women who had come before her, who had faced seemingly insurmountable odds with nothing but faith to guide them.

She thought of her great-grandmother, who had raised seven children alone after her husband was lynched, keeping them fed with nothing but her faith and two strong hands. She remembered her mother, who had put herself through nursing school while battling cancer, her faith never wavering even in her final days.

Opening her eyes, Tanya looked at her reflection in the bathroom mirror. She saw the lines of worry etched on her face and the weariness in her eyes. But beneath that, she saw something else—a divine spark, a strength passed down through generations of Black women who had walked by faith when they couldn't see the way forward.

"Okay, mama," Tanya whispered to her unborn child, placing a hand on her still-flat stomach. "We're going to do this. We're going to walk by faith."

The next few months were a blur of challenges. Tanya slept on friends' couches, took odd jobs, and battled morning sickness while trying to rebuild her life. There were days when she couldn't see how she would make it when the path ahead seemed dark and treacherous.

But each morning, she would place a hand on her growing belly and repeat, "We walk by faith, not by sight." And somehow, step by step, she kept moving forward.

She found a support group for survivors of domestic violence, where she met other Black women who had walked similar paths. Their stories of resilience and triumph became her guideposts, their sisterhood a balm to her wounded spirit.

Through a connection at the support group, Tanya landed a job at a non-profit organization that supports women in crisis. For the first time in years, she felt a sense of purpose beyond survival. She used her struggles to lift other women, turning her pain into power.

As her due date approached, Tanya stood in the nursery she had painstakingly prepared in her small but safe apartment. The crib was secondhand, and the rocking chair was a gift from her support group sisters. It wasn't much, but it was filled with love and hope.

Looking around the room, Tanya marveled at how far she had come. She couldn't have imagined this outcome when she first saw those two pink lines. But she had walked by faith, not sight, and that faith had carried her through the darkness into light.

The first contraction hit just as the sun was rising. As Tanya breathed through the pain, she felt a strength growing within her - the strength of her ancestors, of every Black woman who had brought life into the world against the odds.

Hours later, as she held her daughter for the first time, Tanya felt a profound triumph. She had not only survived but also created new life, hope, and possibilities.

"Welcome to the world, Faith," she whispered to her newborn daughter. "We've got a beautiful journey ahead of us."

As she gazed at her child, Tanya knew there would still be challenges ahead. The path wouldn't always be clear. But she was no longer afraid of the unseen, for she had learned to walk by faith, guided by the wisdom of her foremothers and the strength of her resilient spirit.

At that moment, holding her daughter close, Tanya embodied the triumph of every Black woman over 30 who had faced her fears, reclaimed her power, and stepped into a future bright with promise - walking by faith, transforming struggle into victory with every step.

Prayer:

God, help me to trust in Your plans, even when I cannot see the way forward. Teach me to walk by faith and not sight, knowing that Your guidance is all I need to navigate life's uncertainties.

Affirmation:

I walk by faith, trusting God's perfect plan for my life, even when I cannot see it.

Reflection Questions:

- How do you practice walking by faith rather than sight in your journey?
- Discuss a moment when trusting God's plan was challenging but rewarding.
- How can you incorporate the principle of this scripture into your daily routine?
- How does the affirmation "I trust God's plan for my life" guide you through uncertain times?

Notes:

DAY 6

Scripture: Proverbs 3:5-6

"Trust in the LORD with all your heart and lean not on your understanding; in all your ways submit to him, and he will make your paths straight."

Devotional:

Dr. Zora Williams stood frozen in the middle of her empty classroom, staring at the email on her phone. After 15 years of dedicated service, budget cuts eliminated her position at the historically Black college. At 42, Zora felt the ground shift beneath her feet. This job wasn't just her career; it was her calling, her way of uplifting the next generation of Black scholars.

As panic and anger warred within her, Zora's grandmother's voice echoed in her mind, reciting the verses she'd heard countless times growing up:

"Trust in the Lord with all your heart,

and lean not on your understanding.

in all your ways submit to him,

and he will make your paths straight."

Zora took a deep breath, her hand instinctively reaching for the well-worn Bible in her desk drawer. She opened it to Proverbs 3:5-6, tracing the familiar words with her finger.

"Alright, Lord," she whispered, her voice shaky but resolute. "I don't understand this, but I'm trusting You. Show me the way forward."

The next few months were a whirlwind of job applications, rejections, and soul-searching. Zora found herself questioning everything she thought she knew about her path. Had she been wrong to dedicate her life to academia? Was it time to pivot to a more lucrative career?

But each time doubt crept in, Zora returned to those verses. She joined a prayer group with other Black women facing career transitions, finding strength in their shared faith and experiences. They reminded each other to trust God's plan, even when the path seemed unclear.

One evening, while volunteering at a community center – something she'd started doing to fill her unexpected free time – Zora overheard two teenage girls discussing their struggles with math. Without thinking, she offered to help. Zora felt a familiar spark ignite as she broke down complex concepts into understandable pieces.

The girls' eyes lit up with understanding, and one of them exclaimed, "Dr. Williams, you should be a teacher!"

Zora laughed, explaining that she had been a professor. But as the words left her mouth, a new idea began to form. Maybe her path wasn't meant to be in higher education. Her skills and passion could have an even more significant impact earlier in students' lives.

With renewed purpose, Zora began exploring opportunities in secondary education. She discovered a pilot program to bring experienced educators into underfunded urban schools. The position offered less prestige and a lower salary than her previous job, but as Zora prayed about it, she felt a sense of peace she hadn't experienced in months.

Taking a leap of faith, Zora applied and was accepted into the program. On her first day at the inner-city high school, she stood before a class of skeptical teenagers – many of whom reminded her of herself at that age. The challenges were daunting, but Zora felt equipped and called to face them.

As the semester progressed, Zora saw her students begin to flourish. She introduced college prep programs, mentored aspiring first-generation students, and watched young minds awaken to their potential. The work was more challenging than anything she'd done before but more rewarding.

One afternoon, as Zora was packing up to leave, she noticed a sticky note one of her students had left on her desk. It read: "Thank you for believing in us, Dr. Williams. You're changing lives." Tears welled in Zora's eyes as she recalled her devastation when she lost her college position. She could never have imagined that that painful detour would lead her here, to a place where she could have such a profound impact.

Zora closed her eyes, whispering a prayer of gratitude. "Thank you, Lord, for straightening my path when I couldn't see the way. Thank you for teaching me to trust in You." As she left the school, Zora felt a deep sense of peace and purpose. By trusting in the Lord and submitting to His guidance, she found her way to where she needed to be. Her path hadn't just been straightened; it had been elevated, allowing her to lift a new generation of Black scholars in ways she never imagined.

Zora's story became a testament to the power of faith and trust, inspiring other Black women to hold onto hope in the face of unexpected detours, knowing that sometimes, what looks like a setback is God setting the stage for an even greater triumph.

Prayer:

Lord, I trust you with all my heart. When unsure which direction to take, guide me and make my paths straight. Help me to lean on Your wisdom rather than on my limited understanding.

Affirmation:

I trust in God's wisdom and guidance, and God directs my paths with love and purpose.

Reflection Questions:

- What does trusting in God with all your heart look like for you?
- How has acknowledging God in all your ways impacted your decisions and path in life?
- What are some barriers to fully trusting God, and how do you overcome them?
- Reflect on the affirmation "God directs my steps" and share how this belief shapes your actions and outlook.

Notes:

DAY 7

Scripture: Romans 8:28

"And we know that in all things, God works for the good of those who love him, who have been called according to his purpose."

Devotional:

Ebony sank into her worn armchair, her body heavy with exhaustion and grief. At 50, she found herself starting over – again. The startup she'd poured her life savings into had just folded, leaving her with mountains of debt and a shattered dream. Her marriage had crumbled under the strain, and her adult children were distant, struggling with their challenges.

As tears slid down her cheeks, Ebony's eyes fell on the faded needlepoint hanging on her wall – a gift from her late grandmother. It read: *"And we know that in all things God works for the good of those who love him, who have been called according to his purpose."* - Romans 8:28

Ebony had always found comfort in this verse, but tonight, it felt like a hollow promise. How could any good come from this mess?

As if in answer, her phone buzzed. It was a text from her best friend Aisha: "Sister, remember Romans 8:28. God's not finished with your story yet."

Ebony closed her eyes, letting the familiar words wash over her. She thought about the generations of Black women in her family who had clung to this promise through slavery, Jim Crow, and countless personal trials. Their faith had been a lifeline, a source of strength and hope when all seemed lost.

Taking a deep breath, Ebony decided to do something she hadn't done in years. She pulled out her grandmother's old sewing box and began to stitch. As her fingers worked, memories flooded back—of summer afternoons spent learning to quilt and of the stories her grandmother told about their ancestors' resilience.

Days turned into weeks, and Ebony found solace in her sewing. She started creating beautiful, intricate quilts that told stories of struggle, triumph, faith, and perseverance. When Aisha suggested she sell them online, Ebony hesitated but decided to try it.

To her surprise, orders started pouring in. Women from all over—especially Black women—resonated with the stories woven into each quilt. Ebony found herself selling quilts and sharing wisdom, offering hope, and building a community.

As her business grew, Ebony began teaching quilting classes at the local community center. Many of her students were women facing life transitions—job losses, divorces, and health crises. Together, they stitched and shared, finding healing in the process.

One day, as Ebony was preparing for class, her daughter called. "Mom," she said, her voice thick with emotion, "I just wanted to say I'm proud of you. Seeing you rebuild your life has inspired me to make some changes."

Tears of joy streamed down Ebony's face as she realized her journey wasn't just about her anymore. It touched lives, bringing healing and inspiring others to persevere.

A few months later, Ebony stood before a crowd at a women's empowerment conference, a quilt draped over her shoulders like a cape. As she shared her story – of loss, resilience, and unexpected new beginnings – she saw heads nodding and tears flowing.

"Sisters," she said, her voice strong and clear, "our lives are like this quilt. Each patch represents a trial, a triumph, a moment of grace. We may not always understand the pattern as it's being stitched, but God sees the full design. And God is working all things – even the painful, messy things – for our good."

As applause filled the room, Ebony felt a profound sense of gratitude wash over her. The business failure that had seemed like the end of everything had been the beginning of something beautiful. It had led her back to her roots, to a gift she'd almost forgotten she possessed. It opened doors to touch lives in ways she never imagined.

At that moment, Ebony understood Romans 8:28 in a new and more profound way. God hadn't just worked things out for her good – God had taken the broken pieces of her life and created a masterpiece, a tapestry of grace that was bringing hope and healing to others.

As she looked out at the sea of faces—Black women of all ages, each with their own stories of struggle and strength—Ebony silently renewed her commitment to trust God's plan, even when she couldn't see the whole picture. For she now knew, without a doubt, that God was weaving something beautiful from every thread of her life—the dark and the bright.

Prayer:

Thank You, God, for working all things together for my good. Help me see Your hand in every situation and trust that You are using everything I experience to mold me into the person You've called me to be.

Affirmation:

Everything works together for my good because I am called according to God's purpose.

Reflection Questions:

- How do you find purpose in your challenges, knowing God works for your good?
- How has this scripture helped you trust God's bigger plan for your life?
- How can this verse inspire you to encourage other Black women to see the good in their situations?
- What does the affirmation "Everything works for my good" mean to you, and how does it influence your perspective on life's events?

Notes:

DAY 8

Scripture: Romans 8:35

"Who shall separate us from the love of Christ? Shall trouble, hardship, persecution, famine, nakedness, danger, or sword?"

Devotional:

Amara stood before the mirror in her small apartment, carefully wrapping her hair in a vibrant head wrap. The bold Ankara print was a gift from her late mother, a piece of home she always carried with her. As she adjusted the fabric, Amara's eyes fell on the scripture tattooed on her wrist:

"Who shall separate us from the love of Christ? Shall trouble or hardship or persecution or famine or nakedness or danger or sword?" - Romans 8:35

A sad smile crossed her face as she remembered the day she got the tattoo. It was right after her mother's funeral, a reminder of the faith that had sustained their family through generations of struggle.

Today, Amara needed that reminder more than ever. In a few hours, she stood before the board of directors at the tech company where she worked, pitching her innovative project. As one of the few Black women in a leadership position, Amara knew the stakes were high. She had faced subtle discrimination and doubts about her capabilities throughout her career.

As she gathered her materials, Amara's phone buzzed with a message from her grandmother: "Remember who you are, child. You come from a long line of warriors. No trouble or hardship can separate you from God's love. Go show them what you're made of."

Amara took a deep breath, drawing strength from her grandmother's words and the generations of strong Black women who had paved the way for her. She thought of her great-great-grandmother, who had taught herself to read by candlelight after long days in the fields, and her grandmother, who had marched for civil rights and never lost faith in the face of violence. Her mother, who had worked three jobs to put Amara through college, always reminded her that she was destined for greatness.

As Amara walked into the boardroom, head held high, she felt the weight of their sacrifices and the power of their prayers. The room fell silent as she began her presentation, her voice clear and confident. Halfway through, one of the executives interrupted with a dismissive comment, questioning her data and expertise. For a moment, Amara felt her confidence waver. But then she felt a warmth on her wrist as if her tattoo was coming to life, reminding her of the unbreakable love that sustained her.

Amara addressed the executive's concerns with renewed strength, her knowledge and passion shining through. She wove in stories of how her project would benefit underserved communities, drawing on her experiences and the wisdom passed down through her culture.

As she concluded her presentation, Amara saw a shift in the room. Even the skeptical executive nodded in approval. The CEO stood up, a smile on his face. "Ms. Johnson," he said, "that was exceptional. I think we've found our next big innovation."

Relief and joy washed over Amara as she left the boardroom, her project approved, and her position in the company elevated. As she walked to her office, she overheard two young Black interns whispering excitedly about her success. Amara paused, turning to the young women. "Ladies," she said warmly, "do you have a moment? I'd love to chat with you about your aspirations here."

Over cups of tea, Amara shared her journey with the interns, speaking openly about the challenges she'd faced and the faith that had carried her through. She told them about the strength she drew from her cultural heritage and the importance of lifting others as you climb.

"Remember," she said, showing them her tattoo, "nothing can separate you from God's love. Not hardship, persecution, or doubts others may try to plant in your mind. You are here because you belong here and have the power to change this industry."

Amara felt a deep sense of purpose as the young woman left her office, eyes shining with newfound determination. She realized that her success wasn't just about personal achievement – it was about opening doors and being a living testament to the resilience of Black women.

That evening, as Amara lit her ancestor candle and said her prayers, she felt a profound connection to the generations of women before her. Their strength flowed through her veins, their wisdom guided her steps, and their unshakeable faith in God's love gave her the courage to face any challenge.

"Thank you," she whispered, gently touching her tattoo. "For the love that never let's go, for the culture that lifts me, and for the faith that lights my way."

Amara knew there would be more obstacles ahead and more battles to fight. But she also knew, with unwavering certainty, that she was equipped to face them all. For she was loved with an everlasting love, rooted in a rich heritage, and part of a sisterhood of Black women who had always found a way to rise, thrive, and change the world—no matter what stood in their way.

Prayer:

Lord Jesus, thank you for your unending love that nothing can separate us from. Help us to rest in the assurance of your love, especially when we feel alone or unworthy. May we always remember that your love is constant and perfect. In your name, Amen.

Affirmation:

I am deeply loved and valued by Christ. Nothing can separate me from God's unwavering love.

Reflection Questions:

- How does the assurance that nothing can separate us from God's love impact your identity as a Black woman?
- What specific challenges to Black women might threaten your relationship with God, and how does this verse speak to those fears?
- How can you remind yourself of God's unshakeable love during racial injustice or personal trials?
- How can the community of Black women uplift each other in the knowledge of God's inseparable love?

Notes:

DAY 9

Scripture: Romans 12:2

"Do not conform to the pattern of this world but be transformed by the renewing of your mind. Then, you can test and approve what God's will is—his good, pleasing, and perfect will."

Devotional:

Kendra stared at her reflection in the mirror, barely recognizing the woman looking back at her. At 45, she had achieved everything society told her she should want - a high-powered corporate job, a luxury apartment in the city, designer clothes, and a busy social life. Yet, she felt empty, constantly chasing the next promotion, the next achievement, the next fleeting moment of validation.

A small, framed cross-stitch caught her eye as she applied another layer of makeup, preparing for another long day at the office. It was a gift from her late aunt, with the words of Romans 12:2 carefully stitched:

"Do not conform to the pattern of this world but be transformed by the renewing of your mind. Then you can test and approve what God's will is—his good, pleasing, and perfect will."

Kendra had always admired her Aunt Bessie, a pillar of their community who seemed to radiate joy despite living a life that the world might consider ordinary. Looking at those words, Kendra felt a stirring in her soul.

That evening, instead of attending yet another networking event, Kendra dug out her old Bible. As she reread Romans 12:2, she realized how much she had conformed to the world's expectations, losing sight of God's purpose for her life.

Determined to make a change, Kendra began a journey of renewing her mind. She started small, setting aside time each morning for prayer and Bible study. She joined a women's group at her church, connecting with other Black women seeking to align their lives with God's will.

As weeks turned into months, Kendra noticed subtle changes. She was less concerned with impressing others and more focused on serving her community. She started volunteering at a local youth center, mentoring young girls from underprivileged backgrounds.

One day, as Kendra was leaving work, her boss called her into his office. "Kendra," he said, "I've noticed a change in you lately. You seem... different. More confident, more purposeful. What's your secret?" Kendra smiled, realizing this was an opportunity to share her faith. She told him about her transformation journey, about renewing her mind with God's Word and seeking His will for her life.

To her surprise, her boss listened intently. "You know," he said thoughtfully, "we've been looking for someone to head up our new community outreach initiative. I think you'd be perfect for it." Kendra felt a surge of excitement. This was an opportunity to align her work with her newfound purpose, to use her skills and experience to make a real difference in people's lives.

As she embarked on this new role, Kendra faced challenges she never would have imagined tackling. But with each obstacle, she returned to Romans 12:2, reminding herself to seek God's will and not conform to the world's expectations.

One year into her new position, Kendra stood before a group of young women at the youth center's career day. As she shared her story of transformation, she saw hope ignite in their eyes.

"Ladies," she said, her voice strong and clear, "the world will try to mold you into what it thinks you should be. But I'm here to tell you that true fulfillment comes from allowing God to transform you from the inside out. It's about renewing your mind with His truth and living out His purpose for your life."

After her speech, a young girl approached her, eyes shining. "Ms. Kendra," she said shyly, "I want to be like you when I grow up—not just successful but making a difference."

Kendra felt tears prick her eyes as she hugged the girl. She realized that her transformation hadn't just changed her life - it was having a ripple effect, touching the lives of others in ways she never could have imagined.

That night, as Kendra sat in her living room - no longer the sterile, showroom-perfect space it once was, but warm and inviting, often filled with laughter from church friends and mentees - she reflected on her journey.

She picked up the framed cross-stitch, tracing the words of Romans 12:2 with her finger. What had started as a small act of obedience - choosing to renew her mind with God's Word - had led to a complete transformation of her life, purpose, and impact on the world.

Kendra realized that true freedom wasn't found in conforming to the world's standards but in allowing God to transform her into the woman He had created her to be. In that transformation, she had not only found fulfillment but had also become a catalyst for change in her community.

As she closed her eyes in prayer, Kendra felt a deep sense of peace and purpose. She was no longer conformed to the pattern of this world. Instead, she was transformed and renewed and lived out God's good, pleasing, and perfect will for her life.

Prayer:

Father, we ask for Your help in renewing our minds daily. Help us to resist conforming to the world's standards and instead be transformed by Your Word. Guide us to understand and follow Your will for our lives. In Jesus' name, Amen.

Affirmation:

The renewing of my mind transforms me daily. God's will guide my path, not the world's standards.

Reflection Questions:

- What does it mean to you to resist conforming to societal standards, especially as a Black woman today?
- How can you transform your mind daily to align more closely with God's will for your life?
- What practical steps can you take to renew your mind when faced with negative stereotypes or cultural pressures?
- How does embracing your unique identity as a Black woman contribute to the transformation and renewal of your mind?

Notes:

DAY 10

Scripture: Psalm 43:5

"Why, my soul, are you downcast? Why so disturbed within me? Put your hope in God, for I will yet praise him, my Savior and my God."

Devotional:

Maya's fingers hovered over the piano keys, trembling slightly. The once-familiar ivory felt foreign under her touch. It had been months since she'd played – months since the accident that had taken her husband and left her world in shambles.

At 52, Maya found herself a widow, and her dreams of growing old together instantly shattered. The church she'd once filled with soulful gospel music now echoed silently. Her spirit, once buoyant with faith and joy, felt weighed down by grief and despair. As she sat at the piano in her empty living room, Maya's eyes fell on the framed scripture on the wall – a gift from her late husband on their last anniversary:

"Why, my soul, are you downcast? Why so disturbed within me? Put your hope in God, for I will yet praise him, my Savior and my God." - Psalm 43:5

The words blurred as tears filled her eyes. How could she praise God when her heart was broken? How could she find hope when her future seemed so bleak?

Just then, her phone buzzed with a message from Sister Beatrice, the church's oldest member: "Child, we miss your music. Remember, even in the valley, there's a song to be sung."

Maya closed her eyes, letting the familiar words of Psalm 43:5 wash over her. She thought of her grandmother, who had sung spirituals while working in the fields, finding strength in praise even amidst hardship. She remembered her mother, humming hymns as she marched for civil rights, her faith unshaken by the violence she faced.

Taking a deep breath, Maya placed her fingers on the keys and began to play. The melody was hesitant at first, a simple hymn she'd known since childhood. As she played, she started to hum, then to sing softly:

"Put your hope in God, for I will yet praise Him..."

Her voice grew stronger with each word. Tears flowed freely now, but they were no longer just tears of sorrow. They were tears of release, surrender, and a soul choosing to hope despite the pain.

As Maya continued to play and sing, she felt a shift within her. The weight of despair began to lift, replaced by a fragile but growing sense of peace. She wasn't denying her grief or pretending everything was fine. Instead, she was choosing to anchor her soul in something—someone—greater than her circumstances.

The following Sunday, Maya returned to church for the first time since the funeral. Sitting in her usual spot by the piano, she felt a gentle nudge from the Holy Spirit. With trembling legs, she stood and walked to the front.

"Sisters and brothers," she said, her voice quavering but determined, "I've been in a dark valley these past months. But there's a scripture that's been speaking to my heart." She shared Psalm 43:5, her voice growing stronger as she spoke.

"I don't have all the answers," Maya continued, "and some days, the pain is still overwhelming. But I'm choosing to put my hope in God. And today, I want to praise God, not because everything is okay, but because God is faithful even when things are not okay."

As Maya began to play and sing, her rich contralto filling the sanctuary, she saw tears in the eyes of her church family. Many had experienced their valleys of despair, and her vulnerability touched a chord in their hearts.

In the weeks and months that followed, Maya found herself on a journey of healing. There were still difficult days, moments when her soul felt downcast. But she returned to Psalm 43:5 each time, choosing to put her hope in God and offer praise even when she didn't feel like it.

Slowly but surely, Maya's music ministry was reborn. But it was different now – more profound, more soulful. Her songs spoke not just of joy but of hope amid sorrow, of faith that endures through life's storms.

One year after the accident, Maya stood before a crowd at a women's conference, her fingers dancing over the keys as she shared her testimony through song. As she sang the words of Psalm 43:5, she saw heads nodding and hands raising in agreement.

"Sisters," she said, pausing in her music, "life will bring valleys. There will be times when your soul feels downcast and disturbed. But in those moments, remember to anchor your hope in God. Choose to praise God, not because of your circumstances, but because of who God is. And in that praise, you'll find the strength to keep going."

As Maya resumed playing, her music swelling with hope and praise, she realized that her journey through grief had led her to a deeper understanding of God's faithfulness. Her praise was no longer just a habit or a performance – it was a lifeline, a declaration of hope, a melody that could pierce through even the darkest night.

In helping others find hope through her music and testimony, Maya had found healing for her soul. She was living proof that a song would be sung even in the deepest valley—a melody of hope that could lift the downcast soul and restore the weary spirit.

Prayer:

Dear God, thank You for being our source of hope and strength. When our souls are downcast, remind us to put our hope in You and praise Your name. Fill us with Your joy and peace as we trust in You. In Jesus' name, Amen.

Affirmation:

My hope is in God, and God fills me with joy and peace. I will praise God in all circumstances.

Reflection Questions:

- How do you navigate feelings of despair or discouragement as a Black woman, and how does this verse guide you to hope in God?
- How can you actively praise God even when facing challenges specific to your identity and experiences?
- How does this verse encourage you to speak to your soul and affirm your faith in God's promises?
- How can you find hope and strength in God's presence despite the pressures or pains of life as a Black woman?

Notes:

DAY 11

Scripture: John 10:10

"The thief comes only to steal, kill, and destroy; I have come that they may have life and have it to the full."

Devotional:

Jasmine's stilettos clicked against the polished floor of her corner office, each step echoing the hollow feeling in her chest. At 38, she had climbed to the top of the corporate ladder, her designer wardrobe and luxury car the envy of her colleagues. Yet, as she stared at the city skyline, she felt an overwhelming sense of emptiness.

She had relentlessly chased success, believing it would fill the void she'd carried since childhood. Growing up in a rough neighborhood, Jasmine had vowed to escape poverty and prove her worth to the world. But now, having achieved everything she'd dreamed of, she found herself more lost than ever.

That evening, Jasmine wandered into a small church near her office instead of heading to her usual happy hour. She hadn't stepped foot in a place of worship since she was a child, dragged along by her grandmother. As she sat in the back pew, the Pastor's words cut through her internal turmoil:

"The thief comes only to steal and kill and destroy; I have come that they may have life, and have it to the full." - John 10:10

Jasmine felt as if the words were speaking directly to her soul. She realized that in her pursuit of success, she had allowed the "thief" – societal expectations, her ambitions, or the wounds of her past – to steal her joy and destroy her peace.

After the service, Jasmine approached the Pastor, her usual confidence replaced by vulnerability. "What does it mean to have life to the full?" she asked, her voice barely above a whisper.

The Pastor, an older Black woman with kind eyes, smiled warmly. "Child, it means living in the abundance of God's love and purpose for your life. It's not about what you have, but about who you are in God."

Those words sparked a journey of transformation for Jasmine. She began attending Bible study, rediscovering the faith of her childhood but seeing it with new eyes. She learned that the abundant life Jesus promised wasn't about material wealth but about spiritual richness – peace that surpasses understanding, joy that doesn't depend on circumstances, and love that knows no bounds.

As Jasmine deepened her relationship with God, she felt a shift in her priorities. She started volunteering at a youth center in her old neighborhood, mentoring young girls who reminded her of herself. For the first time, she felt a sense of purpose beyond her success.

Jasmine felt a surge of excitement. This was an opportunity to align her work with her newfound purpose, to use her skills and experience to make a real difference in people's lives.

As she embarked on this new role, Jasmine faced challenges she never imagined tackling. But with each obstacle, she returned to John 10:10, reminding herself of the abundant life Christ had promised—a life not defined by external success but by internal peace and purpose.

Prayer:

Lord Jesus, thank You for offering us abundant life. Help us to seek fulfillment in You alone and to experience the fullness of life that You promise. Lead us to live with purpose and joy, reflecting Your love to those around us. In Your name, Amen.

Affirmation:

I live an abundant life through Christ. My life is filled with God's presence, purpose, and joy.

Reflection Questions:

- How do you interpret the promise of abundant life in the context of your experiences as a Black woman?
- What are some things that may try to "steal, kill, or destroy" your joy, and how does Jesus' promise of life counteract those threats?
- How can you embrace the fullness of life Jesus offers, particularly in a society that may undervalue your worth?
- How can you share this promise of abundant life with other Black women in your community?

Notes:

DAY 12

Scripture: Colossians 1:13-14

"For he has rescued us from the dominion of darkness and brought us into the kingdom of the Son he loves, in whom we have redemption, the forgiveness of sins."

Devotional:

Sarah slumped against the cold brick wall of her apartment, her head in her hands. The weight of her past mistakes pressed down on her like a physical force, threatening to crush her spirit entirely. Years of poor choices, broken relationships, and a life spiraling out of control had left her feeling trapped in a prison of her own making.

She thought back to the string of bad decisions that had led her here: the lies she'd told to cover up her addiction, the trust she'd betrayed, the opportunities she'd squandered. Each memory was a fresh wound, reopening the deep well of shame within her.

"I'm too far gone," Sarah whispered, tears streaming down her face. "How could anyone forgive me after everything I've done?"

As she sat there, drowning in her despair, her eyes fell on the small Bible her grandmother had given her years ago. It lay on her nightstand, untouched for so long. She reached for it with trembling hands, feeling a faint glimmer of hope stirring in her heart.

The pages fell open to Colossians, and her gaze was drawn to Chapter 1, verses 13 and 14:

"For he has rescued us from the dominion of darkness and brought us into the kingdom of the Son he loves, in whom we have redemption, the forgiveness of sins."

The words pierced through the fog of guilt and shame that had clouded Sarah's mind for so long. She read them again and again, letting their truth sink deep into her soul.

"Rescued from the dominion of darkness," she murmured, her voice growing stronger. "Brought into His kingdom."

Sarah felt a spark of hope ignite within her for the first time in years. The realization dawned that her past didn't have to define her future. God's forgiveness was more significant than her mistakes, and His love was more powerful than her shame.

With tears of relief now flowing, Sarah closed her eyes and prayed. "God, I've been living in darkness for so long. Please rescue me. I want to live in Your light."

At that moment, Sarah felt as if a heavy burden had been lifted from her shoulders. The chains of guilt that had bound her for so long began to loosen. She wasn't instantly free from all her struggles, but she had taken the first step on a new path of redemption, forgiveness, and grace.

As days turned weeks and weeks into months, Sarah's life began to transform. She sought help for her addiction, made amends where she could, and surrounded herself with a supportive community of faith. There were still challenges and moments of doubt, but she clung to the truth of Colossians 1:13-14, reminding herself daily of God's redemptive power.

Sarah's past no longer held her captive. Instead, it became a testimony to God's incredible grace and transformative power. She had been rescued from the domain of darkness and was learning, day by day, to walk in the light of God's kingdom.

Prayer:

God, thank you for rescuing us from darkness and bringing us into your kingdom. Thank you for your forgiveness and redemption. Help us to live in the freedom and grace you have given us, leaving our past behind and walking in your light. In Jesus' name, Amen.

Affirmation:

I am redeemed and forgiven by God. I walk in God's light and grace, free from my past.

Reflection Questions:

- How does knowing that you have been rescued from darkness influence your understanding of freedom as a Black woman?
- What does redemption through Christ mean to you personally, especially in the face of historical and current racial injustices?
- How can you live out the reality of being part of God's Kingdom in your daily life as a Black woman?
- How does this passage encourage you to view your past, present, and future in the light of God's redemption?

Notes:

DAY 13

Scripture: 2 Thessalonians 3:3

"But the Lord is faithful, and he will strengthen you and protect you from the evil one."

Devotional:

Mia sat in her car, gripping the steering wheel so tightly that her knuckles turned white. The shelter's parking lot was quiet except for the distant sound of traffic, but her mind was a storm. She wasn't sure if her legs would even work if she tried to step out.

She glanced at the rearview mirror, catching sight of the faint bruise on her cheek. It had faded some since last week, but the memory of how it got there hadn't. Her ex had always known how to make her feel small and wield his words like weapons, even when his hands stayed at his sides. But last time? Last time, it had been different.

It was why she'd packed everything she could into two garbage bags and taken off in the middle of the night. She'd left behind the house. The life. The "perfect" image. And now, she was, sitting in the parking lot of a place she never thought she'd need.

Mia closed her eyes and let out a shaky breath. "God," she whispered, "I don't even know if you're listening right now. But I'm scared. I don't know what's next and feel like I'm falling apart."

She sat in silence, the weight of her fear pressing down on her like a heavy blanket. And then, almost imperceptibly, a thought rose in her mind. It wasn't loud or dramatic—just a quiet reassurance, like a voice carried on the wind:

"But the Lord is faithful, and he will strengthen you and protect you from the evil one."

The words hit her like a lifeline, momentarily pulling her out of the spiral. She remembered hearing it once at church, back when she used to go. Back when her life felt steady.

Mia opened her eyes and stared at the shelter's front door. It was just a building—nothing special, really—but in that moment, it felt like a fortress. A place where she could catch her breath. A place where she could start over.

She thought about the years she'd spent feeling like she had to fight every battle alone. How she'd convinced herself that she was the only one who could protect herself, even when it was clear she couldn't. But sitting here now, she realized she might not have to do it alone.

Maybe God really was faithful. Maybe God really could protect her. Mia wiped her eyes, took a deep breath, and opened the car door. Her legs felt wobbly as she stood up, but each step toward the shelter felt steadier than the last.

When she reached the door, a woman inside opened it with a warm smile. "Welcome," she said softly, her voice full of kindness. Mia nodded, her voice catching in her throat. "Thank you," she managed to say.

As she stepped inside, a strange feeling washed over her. It wasn't that all her fear disappeared; it was still lingering in the background. But she felt something stronger than the fear for the first time in a long time.

She felt hope. And as she walked deeper into the shelter, she whispered, "Thank you, God." Because for the first time, she believed it: the Lord was faithful. And He wasn't going to let her face this alone.

Prayer:

Lord, thank You for Your faithfulness and protection. Strengthen us and guard us from all evil. Help us to trust in Your unwavering presence and find peace in Your protection. In Jesus' name, Amen.

Affirmation:

God is my protector and strength. I face my fears with confidence in God's faithfulness.

Reflection Questions:

- What comfort do you find in God's faithfulness to protect you from evil, particularly in challenging circumstances as a Black woman?
- How does this verse strengthen your resolve to stand firm in your faith despite societal pressures?
- How can you lean on God's protection when you feel vulnerable or threatened by external forces?
- How can you encourage other Black women to trust God's steadfast protection and faithfulness?

Notes:

DAY 14

Scripture: Jeremiah 29:11

"For I know the plans I have for you," declares the LORD, "plans to prosper you and not to harm you, plans to give you hope and a future."

Devotional:

It was a Saturday afternoon, and the sun poured through the window of Tiana's small apartment, casting streaks of light across her coffee table. The room was quiet except for her speaker's soft hum of gospel music. Tiana sat cross-legged on the floor, surrounded by magazines, scissors, glue sticks, and a big poster board.

She stared at the blank board, her mind as empty as the space before her. The idea of making a vision board had seemed fun when her best friend suggested it last week. But now, sitting here, Tiana didn't even know where to start.

Her life wasn't exactly overflowing with things to celebrate. Three months ago, she had been laid off from her job, and finding something new had been a struggle. The bills were piling up, her car had been acting up, and the cracks in her confidence were starting to feel like they might break her completely.

Tiana sighed and picked up a pair of scissors, flipping through a magazine without much enthusiasm. She paused on an image of a woman smiling in front of a home with a "Sold" sign and rolled her eyes. "Yeah, right," she muttered.

She was about to close the magazine when her phone buzzed. It was a text from her mom:

"Don't forget, baby: God's got a plan for you." Jeremiah 29:11.

Tiana stared at the words for a moment, her chest tightening. That verse—the one her mom had recited over and over growing up—always seemed too big, too lofty. Plans to prosper her? Plans for hope and a future? She couldn't even plan her next meal.

She set the phone down and closed her eyes. "God," she whispered, "I don't see it. I don't see the plan. I'm trying to trust you, but it feels like I'm stuck."

The music in the background shifted to a song her grandma used to hum while cooking: *"His Eye Is on the Sparrow."* And for some reason, as she listened, her heart softened just a little. She thought about her grandma—how she'd raised five kids on her own after her husband passed, working as a seamstress during the day and cleaning offices at night. Grandma had always said it was God who got her through.

Tiana opened her eyes and looked at the blank board again. This time, it didn't feel so intimidating. She reached for another magazine and began cutting out things that spoke to her—not just pictures of what she wanted, but words that reminded her of who she was.

She cut out the word *"Strength "* because black women carried the weight of the world on their shoulders, and she was no different.

She cut out *"Faith."* Because even when life got hard, she knew deep down that God hadn't forgotten her.

She cut out *"Joy"* because she deserved it, even in the middle of the struggle.

As she worked, something shifted inside her. It wasn't like her problems disappeared—her car still needed fixing, and her bank account still looked sad. But for the first time in weeks, she felt a flicker of hope.

By the time she was done, the board was covered with images and words that felt like pieces of her heart. There was a picture of a house because she still dreamed of owning one someday. There was a Black woman in a business suit because she wasn't giving up on her career. And right in the center, the words *"God's Plan"* were in bold letters.

Tiana leaned back and smiled—a small, quiet smile, but a real one. She didn't know what the future held, but she could feel a sense of purpose stirring inside her again.

She propped the vision board up on her dresser and then picked up her phone to text her mom: *"Thanks for the reminder. I needed it today. I love you."*

As she hit send, Tiana whispered, "Alright, God. I'm trusting you with this. I don't know the plan, but I know you do." For the first time in a long time, she believed that God's plans for her were good.

Prayer:

Lord, we thank you for having plans for our lives, plans to prosper us and give us hope and a future. Help us surrender our plans to you, trust in your process, and submit to your will. May we find peace and fulfillment in following your purpose for our lives. In Jesus' name, Amen.

Affirmation:

God's plans for me are to prosper and not to harm me, to give me hope and a future. I surrender, trust, and submit to God's will.

Reflection Questions:

- How does this scripture give you hope for your future?
- Describe a time when you felt uncertain about your future and how this verse brought you comfort.
- How does believing in God's plans for you help you set and achieve personal goals?
- Reflect on the affirmation "God has good plans for me" and how it motivates you to pursue your dreams.

Notes:

DAY 15

Scripture: 2 Timothy 1:7

"For the Spirit God gave us does not make us timid, but gives us power, love and self-discipline."

Devotional:

Kayla sat on the edge of her bed, staring at her phone screen. Her fingers hovered over the keyboard, trembling as she typed, erased, and retyped the same message over and over again.

"I just don't think this is working anymore."

Her heart clenched as she read the words. She knew they were true but sending them felt impossible. She had been with Marcus for three years. Three years of memories, laughter, and love—but also three years of being dismissed, ignored, and made to feel like she wasn't enough.

She'd ignored the red flags for so long, convincing herself that things would get better. But deep down, she knew it wasn't going to change. Marcus wasn't going to change. And staying with him was slowly chipping away at the person she used to be.

Kayla put her phone down and buried her face in her hands. "God," she whispered, her voice shaky, "I can't do this. I don't have the strength to walk away. What if I regret it? What if I'm making a mistake?"

The room was silent except for the hum of the air conditioner. Kayla's thoughts swirled, each one louder than the last.

"You'll never find anyone better."

"What if you end up alone?"

"You're being dramatic—he's not that bad."

As the doubts threatened to overwhelm her, a memory surfaced—her grandma sitting at the kitchen table, her Bible open, her voice steady and sure:

"For the Spirit God gave us does not make us timid, but gives us power, love, and self-discipline."

The words echoed in Kayla's mind, cutting through the noise. Power. Love. Self-discipline.

She sat up straighter, letting the verse settle into her heart. She thought about all the times she'd stayed silent when Marcus dismissed her feelings. All the times she'd let him make her feel small like her dreams and needs didn't matter.

But God didn't call her to live in fear or shrink herself for anyone. The Spirit, He gave her wasn't timid—it was full of power—the power to set boundaries and to walk away from what wasn't good for her.

Kayla picked up her phone again, her hands steadier this time. She read over the message once more, then added a few more words:

"I just don't think this is working anymore. I need time to focus on myself and the life God has for me. I wish you the best, but I can't keep holding on to something that isn't healthy for me."

She hit send before she could second-guess herself. Her heart raced, but instead of regret, she felt a strange sense of relief. Like a weight, she didn't even realize she'd been carrying had finally been lifted.

For the first time in years, Kayla felt free. She set the phone down and looked out the window, the late afternoon sun casting a warm glow over her room. She whispered a quiet prayer: "Thank you, God, for giving me the courage to choose myself. Help me to keep trusting you with what's next."

The Spirit inside her wasn't timid—it was powerful. At that moment, Kayla knew she had made the right choice—not just for her future but also for her peace.

Prayer:

Lord, thank you for empowering us with your spirit of power, love, and a sound mind. Help us to overcome our fears and walk in the confidence that you have given us. May we trust in your strength and love as we pursue the purpose you have for our lives. In Jesus' name, Amen.

Affirmation:

I am empowered by God's spirit of power, love, and a sound mind. I face my fears with confidence and courage.

Reflection Questions:

- Reflect on a time when fear held you back from pursuing something important in your life. How does knowing that God has given you a spirit of power, love, and a sound mind encourage you to face your fears boldly?

- As a Black woman, society may sometimes undermine your strength. How does this verse empower you to embrace and display the God-given power and love within you, even in challenging situations?

- Mental health is crucial for your overall well-being. How can you apply the principle of having a sound mind in your daily life, particularly when dealing with stress, anxiety, or pressure from external expectations?

- How can you use the spirit of power, love, and self-discipline to uplift and support other Black women in your community? Share practical ways you can be a source of strength and encouragement to those around you.

Notes:

DAY 16

Scripture: Psalm 23:1

"The LORD is my shepherd, I lack nothing."

Devotional:

Essence exhaled slowly; her breath visible in the chilly morning air as she locked the door to her small apartment. The weight of uncertainty pressed heavily on her shoulders as she began her walk to the bus stop. At 45, she never imagined she'd be starting over, but life had a way of throwing curveballs.

Six months ago, Essence had lost her job of fifteen years when the company downsized. The severance package had helped for a while, but now her savings were dwindling, and the job market seemed impenetrable. As a single mother with two teenagers to support, the pressure was immense.

As she waited for the bus, Essence closed her eyes and whispered the words her grandmother had taught her long ago: "The Lord is my shepherd; I lack nothing." Psalm 23:1 had been a cornerstone of her faith since childhood, but now it felt like a lifeline.

The bus ride to her temporary job at a local diner was filled with worried thoughts. Would this be enough to keep a roof over their heads? How would she afford Jamal's college applications or Aisha's dance lessons? The questions swirled in her mind, threatening to overwhelm her.

As Essence tied on her apron at the diner, she overheard two regular customers discussing a new community center opening up in their neighborhood. They mentioned needing someone with experience in youth programs and community outreach.

Essence's heart quickened. Before her corporate job, she had worked extensively with youth programs at her church. Could this be an opportunity? Or was she grasping at straws?

Throughout her shift, Essence repeated, "The Lord is my shepherd." Each time she said it, a sense of calm washed over her. She remembered how unexpected blessings had often appeared just when she needed them most throughout her life.

After her shift, mustering all her courage, Essence approached the customers and inquired about the community center position. To her surprise, one of them was on the hiring committee and offered to set up an interview on the spot.

As Essence shared her experience and passion for community work, she felt a familiar warmth in her chest – the same feeling she got when reciting Psalm 23:1. It was as if the Shepherd was gently guiding her path, leading her to still waters in the midst of her storm.

Two weeks later, Essence stood in front of a mirror, adjusting her blazer before her first day as the new Community Outreach Coordinator. The job offered better pay and benefits, and most importantly, it aligned with her heart for service.

Tears of gratitude welled in her eyes as she thought about the journey. The uncertainty and fear had been fundamental but so had the provision and guidance of her Shepherd. Essence realized that "I shall not want" didn't mean she would never face a lack or challenges. Instead, it was a promise that in every season, her Shepherd would provide – sometimes in ways she least expected.

As she left for work, Essence paused to write a note for her children: "Trust in the Shepherd, for God will always provide." She smiled, knowing that her story of faith and provision would now become part of their legacy, too.

With a heart full of peace and purpose, Essence stepped out into the morning sunshine. The path ahead was bright, illuminated by the unfailing love of her Shepherd.

Prayer:

God, thank you for being our shepherd and provider. Help us to trust in your provision and guidance, knowing that you care for us and will meet all our needs. May we find peace in your presence and follow your leading. In Jesus' name, Amen.

Affirmation:

The Lord is my shepherd, and I lack nothing. I trust in God's provision and guidance.

Reflection Questions:

- As a Black woman, how does the image of God as a shepherd resonate with your experiences of guidance and protection?
- In what areas of your life do you find it challenging to trust that God will provide for all your needs?
- How can embracing this verse help you navigate the unique pressures and expectations placed on Black women in today's society?
- Reflect on a time when you felt God's shepherding presence during a difficult situation. How did it impact your faith?

Notes:

DAY 17

Scripture: Matthew 6:33

"But seek first his kingdom and his righteousness, and all these things will be given to you as well."

Devotional:

Imani stared at her reflection in the bathroom mirror, barely recognizing the exhausted woman looking back at her. At 35, she had achieved what many would consider success – a thriving career as a marketing executive, two beautiful children, and a supportive husband. Yet, as she rushed to apply her makeup before another hectic day, she felt a gnawing emptiness that no number of professional accolades could fill.

Her phone buzzed incessantly – emails from clients, messages from her children's school, reminders of deadlines and appointments. Imani closed her eyes, trying to center herself, but the quiet moment was fleeting. As she hurried out the door, she caught a glimpse of her Bible on the nightstand, untouched for weeks. A pang of guilt hit her, but she pushed it aside. There was no time for that now.

The day unfolded in its usual chaotic manner. Imani navigated through high-stakes meetings, picked up her kids from after-school activities, and managed to throw together a semblance of dinner. As she collapsed onto the couch that evening, her mother's words echoed in her mind: "Baby, no matter how busy life gets, always seek first the kingdom of God." Imani sighed, remembering the peace she used to feel when her faith was at the center of her life. When had she let the world's demands crowd out her spiritual needs?

That night, unable to sleep, Imani found herself drawn to her Bible. As she opened it, a familiar verse caught her eye –

Matthew 6:33: "But seek first his kingdom and his righteousness, and all these things will be given to you as well."

The words resonated deeply, and Imani felt a stirring in her soul. She realized that in her pursuit of earthly success, she had neglected her spiritual foundation. With tears in her eyes, she made a decision: it was time to realign her priorities.

The following day, instead of immediately checking her emails, Imani woke up early to pray and study her Bible. It felt awkward at first, like reuniting with an old friend after years apart. But as the days passed, she found herself craving this quiet time.

Imani began to make small but significant changes. She joined a women's Bible study group at her church, connecting with other professional women navigating similar challenges. She started volunteering at a local community center, using her marketing skills to help small businesses owned by people of color.

To her surprise, as she devoted more time to her faith, other aspects of her life began to flourish. At work, she found herself approaching challenges with a newfound clarity and purpose. Her creative ideas flowed more freely, and her team responded positively to her more balanced leadership style.

At home, the atmosphere shifted. By starting her day grounded in faith, Imani was more patient with her children and more present with her husband. Family dinners became a time of genuine connection rather than distracted conversation.

One evening, as Imani tucked her daughter into bed, the little girl said, "Mommy, you seem happier now. Is it because you're praying more?" Imani hugged her tightly, realizing that her renewed faith was impacting not just her but her entire family.

Months passed, and while life was still busy, Imani no longer felt overwhelmed. She had learned to filter her decisions through the lens of her faith, often asking herself, "Am I seeking God's kingdom first in this?"

In balancing career, family, and faith, Imani discovered a timeless truth: when you align your life with God's priorities, everything else falls into place—not always easily but always purposefully.

Prayer:

Lord, help me to seek your kingdom first in all that I do. When life becomes overwhelming, remind me that my true success comes from aligning my life with your will. Guide me to put you at the center, trusting that you will provide for all my needs.

Affirmation:

I seek God's kingdom first, knowing that everything else in my life will be added in its perfect time.

Reflection Questions:

- As a Black woman, what does seeking God's kingdom look like in your daily life and community?
- How can prioritizing God's righteousness help you overcome societal pressures and stereotypes?
- In what ways have you seen God provide for you when you've put His priorities first?
- How can this verse inspire Black women to be changemakers in their families, churches, and communities?

Notes:

DAY 18

Scripture: 2 Corinthians 5:17

"Therefore, if anyone is in Christ, the new creation has come: The old has gone, the new is here!"

Devotional:

Rain poured down in sheets as Maya sat in her car, gripping the steering wheel. The church's parking lot was nearly empty, and the glow of the streetlights reflected off the puddles on the ground.

Her heart was pounding. She hadn't stepped foot in a church in years. Not since before everything fell apart. Not since her life had unraveled, piece by piece until she barely recognized the woman staring back at her in the mirror.

Maya looked at her hands. They were steady now, but she could still remember what it felt like when they weren't—when the withdrawals hit when the cravings screamed louder than reason. She could still remember the nights she sat alone in her apartment, a bottle in one hand and a needle in the other, wondering if this was how her story would end.

But it hadn't ended.

It had been six months since she'd checked herself into rehab. Six months of tears, struggle, and fighting to believe that she could have a life beyond the addiction. Her sponsor had told her about this church—how they had a recovery ministry, a place where people like her could find support and hope.

But what if they judged her? What if they saw her as nothing more than a person with an addiction?

She leaned her head against the steering wheel, her breath shaky. "God," she whispered, "I don't know if I belong here.

I don't even know if you want anything to do with me. But I'm trying. I'm trying to believe that I can start over."

The rain softened, and Maya sat up, wiping her eyes. She grabbed her bag and stepped out of the car, the cool air hitting her face as she made her way to the church door.

Inside, the warmth of the building wrapped around her like a blanket. A woman at the entrance greeted her with a kind smile. "Welcome," she said. "Are you here for the recovery group?"

Maya nodded, her voice catching in her throat.

The woman led her to a small room where a circle of chairs had been set up. A dozen people sat there, some holding cups of coffee, others quietly chatting. Maya hesitated in the doorway, feeling like an outsider.

But then she saw the sign on the wall. It read:

"Therefore, if anyone is in Christ, the new creation has come: The old has gone, the new is here!"

The words hit her like a wave. She had heard that verse before, back when she was a kid in Sunday school. But standing here now, it felt like it was written just for her. The old was gone. The mistakes, the shame, the person she used to be—that was all in the past. And in Christ, she was something new.

One of the group members, a man in his fifties with kind eyes, noticed her hesitation and waved her over. "Come on in," he said. "We've all been where you are. You're in the right place."

Maya took a deep breath and stepped into the circle. As she sat down, the group leader began to speak." Before we start, I want to remind everyone of this truth: You are not your past.

Your mistakes do not define you. In Christ, you are a new creation. And today? Today is a new beginning."

Maya felt tears well up in her eyes, but this time, they weren't tears of regret. They were tears of hope. For the first time in years, she believed it. The old was gone. The news had come. And with God's help, she was ready to step into the future He had for her.

Prayer:

God, I thank you for making me a new creation in Christ. Help me to fully embrace my new identity, leaving behind the shame and guilt of my past. Teach me to walk confidently in the new life you've given me.

Affirmation:

I am a new creation in Christ; my past does not define me, and I walk in the freedom of my new life.

Reflection Questions:

- As a Black woman, how does the concept of being a "new creation" in Christ speak to your identity and self-worth?
- In what ways has your faith journey helped you shed harmful beliefs or behaviors from your past?
- How can embracing your identity as a new creation in Christ empower you to confront and overcome racial and gender-based injustices?
- Reflect on how your relationship with Christ has transformed your perspective on your purpose and potential.

Notes:

DAY 19

Scripture: Isaiah 40:8

"The grass withers and the flowers fall, but the word of our God endures forever."

Devotional:

It had been years since Naomi stepped foot in her grandmother's house. After her passing, the family had been too heartbroken to sort through her belongings, leaving the house untouched like a time capsule. Now, with the house finally being sold, it was Naomi's turn to go through the old attic.

The attic smelled of dust and memories, the air heavy with the scent of cedarwood. Naomi sifted through boxes of photo albums, yellowing letters, and old quilts her grandmother had sewn by hand. She was about to call it a day when her hand brushed against something tucked beneath a stack of newspapers.

It was a Bible.

The leather cover was worn and cracked; the edges frayed from years of use. Naomi recognized it immediately—it had been her grandmother's prized possession. She had carried it everywhere, reading from it every morning while sipping her tea.

Naomi sat down on an old wooden trunk and opened the Bible carefully. The pages were thin and delicate, but every corner was alive with her grandmother's handwriting. Notes filled the margins, verses were underlined in faded ink, and sticky notes peeked out from between the pages.

She flipped to a page where a verse had been circled and underlined multiple times. In her grandmother's handwriting, the words read:

"The grass withers and the flowers fall, but the word of our God endures forever."

Naomi traced the words with her finger, her eyes suddenly stinging with tears. She remembered how her grandmother used to quote that verse every time life got hard.

"It's a reminder, baby," her grandmother would say, her voice soft but steady. "Everything in this world is temporary—our troubles, our pain, even our joys. But God's Word? That lasts forever. You can always count on it."

Naomi closed the Bible, clutching it to her chest. Life had been anything but steady lately. She'd lost her job a few months ago, and her relationship had ended shortly after. It felt like the ground beneath her feet was constantly shifting. But holding this Bible now, she felt something she hadn't felt in a long time: peace.

Her grandmother had faced more than her fair share of struggles—raising four kids on her own, working long hours, enduring loss and hardship. But through it all, she had clung to the promises in this book, believing with all her heart that God's Word was unchanging.

Naomi opened the Bible again and began to read. The words felt like water to her dry, weary soul. She stayed in the attic for hours, flipping through the pages, soaking in the verses her grandmother had underlined, the prayers she had written in the margins.

By the time Naomi left the house, the Bible was tucked securely in her bag. It was no longer just a relic of her grandmother's life—it was a lifeline for her own.

As she walked to her car, the words of Isaiah 40:8 echoed in her mind:

"The grass withers and the flowers fall, but the word of our God endures forever."

The world around her might change. Seasons would come and go. But God's Word? It would remain steady, unshaken, a foundation she could always stand on. And for the first time in months, Naomi felt like she could breathe again.

Prayer:

Lord, help me to hold fast to your word, which never changes and never fails. In a world of uncertainty, let me find peace in the knowledge that your promises endure forever. Amen.

Affirmation:

I stand on God's word, which endures forever.

Reflection Questions:

- Eternal Word: How does the promise that "the word of our God will stand forever" bring you comfort in a world that often devalues the voices and experiences of Black women?
- Cultural Legacy: Reflect on how the endurance of God's word parallels the enduring spirit of Black women throughout history. How does this connection strengthen your faith?
- Anchoring in Scripture: In what ways can you make God's word the anchor of your life, especially when facing cultural and societal challenges? How can you encourage other Black women to do the same?
- Passing Down the Word: How can you ensure that the truth of God's enduring word is passed down to

the next generation of Black women? What practical steps can you take to share and teach the Scriptures within your community?

Notes:

DAY 20

Scripture: Daniel 10:12

"Then he continued, "Do not be afraid, Daniel. Since the first day that you set your mind to gain understanding and to humble yourself before your God, your words were heard, and I have come in response to them""

Devotional:

Natalie sat on the edge of her bed, staring at the ceiling. Her Bible lay open beside her, but she didn't have the energy to read it. She had been praying for years—for a breakthrough in her career, for clarity about her purpose, for something to shift in her life.

But nothing seemed to change.

She had been working the same job for six years, barely making enough to cover her bills. The dreams God had placed in her heart—dreams of starting her own business, mentoring young Black girls, and living a life of impact—felt further away than ever.

Natalie let out a heavy sigh. "God," she whispered, "do you even hear me? I've been praying, fasting, and crying out to you, but it feels like you're silent. What am I supposed to do?"

Her phone buzzed, interrupting her thoughts. It was a text from her older sister, Tameka:

"Don't stop praying, sis. God hears you. Read Daniel 10:12 when you get a chance."

Natalie rolled her eyes slightly. Tameka had always sent her Bible verses and encouraged her to keep her faith. But tonight, she wasn't sure she had it in her.

Still, curiosity got the better of her. She picked up her Bible and flipped to the passage. Her eyes scanned the words:

"Do not be afraid, Daniel. Since the first day that you set your mind to gain understanding and to humble yourself before your God, your words were heard, and I have come in response to them."

She reread it; this time slower. *"Since the first day... your words were heard."*

Natalie's breath caught in her throat. The first day. Not the fiftieth day. Not the thousandth day. The *first* day.

Her mind flashed back to all the times she had prayed—on her knees in her bedroom, in the car on her way to work, during quiet moments at her desk. She had always assumed that her prayers were bouncing off the walls, unheard and unanswered.

But this verse said otherwise.

Natalie closed her eyes, letting the words sink in. "You heard me," she whispered. "You heard me all along."

For the first time in months, a spark of hope ignited in her heart. She thought about Daniel—how he had prayed and fasted for weeks, not knowing that God had already sent an answer. The delay wasn't because God hadn't heard him. It was because there was a spiritual battle happening behind the scenes.

Natalie opened her journal and began to write.

"God, I don't know why the breakthrough hasn't come yet. I don't know what battles are being fought in the spiritual realm. But I believe your Word. I believe that you heard me the first time I prayed. I believe that you're working, even when I can't see it."

As she wrote, tears streamed down her face. They weren't tears of frustration this time—they were tears of surrender. She didn't have all the answers, but she didn't need them. What she needed was the assurance that God was with her, that He was listening, that He hadn't forgotten her.

And now, she had it.

The following day, Natalie woke up with a renewed sense of purpose. Her circumstances hadn't changed, but her perspective had. She got up, brewed her coffee, and sat down to pray.

"Lord," she said, "I'm going to keep praying. I'm going to keep believing. Because I know you've heard me. And I know you're working."

Later, she texted Tameka:

"Thank you for the reminder, sis. I needed that. God's been listening all along."

Tameka replied quickly: *"Of course. I've got you. Keep praying—your breakthrough is coming."*

Natalie smiled. She didn't know when the breakthrough would come, but she knew it *would*, and until then, she would keep trusting.

Because from the very first day, God had been listening.

Prayer:

Lord, thank you for hearing my prayers from the very first day. Even when I don't see immediate answers, help me trust that you are at work. Strengthen my faith and perseverance as I continue to seek you.

Affirmation:

God hears my prayers and works on my behalf, even when I cannot see them.

Reflection Questions:

- As a Black woman, how does this verse encourage you when facing challenges or waiting for answers to prayer?
- In what ways can cultivating humility strengthen your relationship with God and others in your community?
- Reflect on a time when you felt God heard and responded to your prayers. How did it impact your faith journey?
- How can this verse inspire Black women to persist in seeking understanding and spiritual growth, even when immediate results aren't visible?

Notes:

DAY 21

Scripture: Lamentations 3: 22-25

"Because of the Lord's great love, we are not consumed,

for his compassions never fail.

23 They are new every morning;

great is your faithfulness.

24 I say to myself, "The Lord is my portion;

therefore, I will wait for him."

25: The Lord is good to those whose hope is in him,

to the one who seeks him;"

Devotional:

Renee sat by the window, watching the first rays of sunlight break through the horizon. The air was still, and the silence of the early morning wrapped around her like a soft blanket. In her hands was the small leather journal she had started keeping after everything in her life had unraveled.

It had been two years since she lost her mother—two years since her marriage fell apart. Two years since she felt like she had been swallowed whole by grief and heartache.

There were days when she couldn't even get out of bed when the weight of it all pressed down on her chest so hard she could barely breathe. She had cried until she had no tears left, whispered prayers into the darkness, and begged God for relief.

And yet, here she was. Still standing and still breathing.

Renee opened her journal and ran her fingers across the words she had written the night before:

"Because of the Lord's great love, we are not consumed."

Her pastor had preached from Lamentations 3 a few weeks ago, but it wasn't until she read the passage herself that the words truly gripped her heart. She had read them over and over again, letting them sink into the deepest parts of her soul.

She picked up her pen and began to write:

"Lord, Your love has carried me through the darkest days of my life. There were moments I thought I wouldn't survive, but Your faithfulness has been my anchor. Each morning, You remind me that I am not consumed. Your mercies are new every day. Thank You for never letting me go."

Renee closed the journal and set it aside. She took a deep breath, letting the sunlight warm her face.

Her mother used to say that the strength of their ancestors ran through her veins—that the resilience of Black women, born from generations of struggle and triumph, was a gift from God. Renee hadn't always believed it. Some days, the pain felt too heavy, the wounds too fresh.

But now, she was starting to see it.

She saw it in the way she rose each day, even when she didn't feel like it. She saw it in the way she still found joy in small things—the laughter of her niece, the smell of fresh coffee, the soft hum of gospel music on Sunday mornings.

It wasn't that the pain had disappeared. It was still there, a quiet ache in the background of her life. But so was God's love. And God's love was immense.

Renee stood and walked to the kitchen, the wooden floor cool beneath her feet. She made herself a cup of tea and stood by the window again, watching the world wake up.

"Because of the Lord's great love, we are not consumed," she whispered, her voice steady.

The words felt like a lifeline, a reminder that no matter how dark the night, the morning always came. And with it, new mercies, new strength, new hope.

Renee didn't know what the future held. There were still unanswered questions, and pieces of her life felt broken. But she knew one thing: God's love would never fail her. And that was enough to keep her going.

As the sun rose higher in the sky, Renee smiled softly. She was still here, standing, and with God's help, she would keep moving forward, one day at a time.

Prayer:

Lord, thank you for your steadfast love that never ceases. In every trial, remind me that your mercies are new every morning. Great is your faithfulness. Amen.

Affirmation: I am renewed each day by God's love and mercy.

Reflection Questions:

- Understanding Mercy: How does the concept of God's mercy, as described in Lamentations 3:22-24, bring comfort during times of racial injustice or personal suffering? How do you see God's mercies renewed in your life daily?
- Cultural Perseverance: The endurance of God's love is a powerful theme in this passage. How does your

cultural heritage help you understand and appreciate the steadfast love of God in times of adversity?
- Hope Amidst Trials: Reflect on a difficult period in your life. How did clinging to the hope in God's faithfulness help you persevere? How can you use this experience to encourage other Black women in their faith journey?
- Daily Renewal: How can you intentionally seek and recognize God's new mercies every day, particularly when facing challenges related to your identity as a Black woman?

Notes:

DAY 22

Scripture: Isaiah 43:19

"See, I am doing a new thing!

Now it springs up; do you not perceive it?

I am making a way in the wilderness

and streams in the wasteland."

Devotional:

Jaime sat on the park bench, the crisp spring air brushing against her cheeks. The trees above her were beginning to bloom, their soft pink blossoms swaying gently in the breeze. She watched as children played on the swings and couples strolled hand in hand.

Her life felt so far removed from the joy and laughter around her.

It had been a year since her divorce—a year of heartbreak, healing, and trying to rebuild a life she barely recognized. Jaime had poured everything into her marriage, only to watch it fall apart. She had told herself she would never love again. The pain of losing someone she had trusted so deeply was too much to risk.

But lately, there was a stirring in her heart. A gentle whisper she couldn't ignore.

That morning, as she sat at her kitchen table with her Bible open, she came across Isaiah 43:19. The words seemed to leap off the page:

"See, I am doing a new thing! Now it springs up; do you not perceive it? I am making a way in the wilderness and streams in the wasteland."

Jaime had read that verse before, but today, it felt personal. God was speaking directly to her, reminding her that her life wasn't over. He was doing something new.

For the first time in a long time, she felt hope.

Jaime opened her journal and wrote the verse at the top of the page. Beneath it, she wrote:

"Lord, I don't know what the 'new thing' is, but I'm ready. Help me to trust You and to see the opportunities You're placing in front of me. Show me the way through this wilderness."

She had closed her journal with a sense of anticipation, and now, sitting in the park, she let herself believe that maybe—just maybe—God was making way for her.

"Excuse me," a voice interrupted her thoughts.

Jaime looked up to see a tall man standing a few feet away, holding a camera. His warm brown eyes crinkled at the edges as he smiled.

"I'm sorry to bother you," he said, "but I'm a photographer, and I'm working on a series about Black women and joy. I couldn't help but notice how peaceful you looked sitting here. Would you mind if I took your photo?"

Jaime blinked, caught off guard.

"Me? Peaceful?" She let out a small laugh. "That's a first."

The man chuckled. "I mean it. There's something about the way you're sitting here like you're soaking it all in. It's beautiful."

Jaime hesitated. She wasn't sure she wanted to be in front of a camera, especially with everything she'd been through. But then she remembered the verse: *"Now it springs up; do you not perceive it?"*

Maybe this was a sign of the new thing God was doing.

"Okay," she said softly.

The man's smile widened. "Thank you. I promise you'll love it."

He introduced himself as Marcus and quickly adjusted his camera. As he snapped a few photos, they began to talk. Jaime told him about her love for nature and how she often came to the park to clear her mind. Marcus shared how he had started his photography business to celebrate the beauty and strength of Black women.

By the time he finished, they were laughing like old friends.

"Thank you for letting me capture this moment," Marcus said. "I'd love to show you the photos when they're ready. Maybe over coffee?"

Jaime felt her cheeks flush. It had been so long since someone had shown her this kind of attention. But there was something about Marcus—his kindness, his sincerity—that put her at ease.

"I'd like that," she said.

As Marcus walked away, Jaime sat back on the bench, her heart lighter than it had been in months. God was doing a new thing. She didn't know where this path would lead, but she was finally ready to follow it.

Each day after that, Jaime began to look for signs of God's new beginnings. She started saying "yes" to opportunities that scared her, reconnecting with friends, and dreaming about the future again.

As she got to know Marcus through coffee dates, long walks, and deep conversations, she realized that God wasn't just making a way in the wilderness; He was creating something beautiful in her life.

The love she thought she'd lost forever was springing up again, this time rooted in hope, faith, and the unshakable belief that God's love never failed.

Prayer:

God, I thank you for the new things you are doing in my life. Open my eyes to see the new opportunities you are bringing my way. Give me the courage to embrace these new beginnings with faith and trust.

Affirmation:

God is doing a new thing in my life, and I am ready to embrace the new opportunities God is bringing my way.

Reflection Questions:

- As a Black woman, how does the promise of God doing a "new thing" resonate with your hopes and dreams?
- In what areas of your life or community do you long to see God make "a way in the wilderness"?

- How can this verse inspire Black women to be agents of positive change and renewal in their spheres of influence?
- Reflect on a time when God brought unexpected blessings or opportunities into your life. How did it strengthen your faith in His ability to make "streams in the wasteland"?

Notes:

DAY 23

Scripture: 1 Peter 2:9

"But you are a chosen people, a royal priesthood, a holy nation, God's special possession, that you may declare the praises of him who called you out of darkness into his wonderful light."

Devotional:

Growing up, Michelle always felt like she was swimming against the current.

In her predominantly white school, she was often the only Black girl in the classroom. She'd hear the whispers behind her back, endure the stares when she raised her hand, and feel the weight of low expectations from teachers who didn't believe in her potential.

At home, her mother always told her, "Baby, you're fearfully and wonderfully made. Don't you ever let this world tell you otherwise?" But it was hard for Michelle to believe that when the world seemed determined to make her feel small.

As she grew older, the challenges only deepened. Being a Black woman in corporate spaces came with its own set of battles. She constantly felt the need to prove herself, to work twice as hard to be seen as half as good. Even in church, where she should have felt safe, she sometimes felt out of place, wondering if her voice or her perspective truly mattered.

One Sunday, after a tough week at work, Michelle sat in the back pew of her church, feeling drained and defeated. The choir sang a hymn about God's faithfulness, but she barely heard the words. Her heart felt heavy, weighed down by the lies she had been fighting her whole life—the ones that told her she wasn't enough.

As the pastor began his sermon, he read from 1 Peter 2:9:

"But you are a chosen generation, a royal priesthood, a holy nation, God's special possession, that you may declare the praises of Him who called you out of darkness into His marvelous light."

Michelle sat up a little straighter. She had heard that verse before, but something about it hit differently this time.

"You are chosen," the pastor said. "You are royalty. You are God's special possession. That's who you are. Don't let anyone or anything tell you otherwise."

The words sank deep into Michelle's spirit. A lump rose in her throat, and tears stung her eyes.

Chosen. Royal. God's special possession.

For so long, she had let the world define her—by her skin color, her gender, and her struggles. But in that moment, she realized the truth: her identity wasn't rooted in what the world said about her. It was rooted in what God said about her.

When the service ended, Michelle went home and opened her Bible to 1 Peter 2:9. She read the verse again and again, letting it wash over her. She grabbed her journal and began to write:

"God, thank You for choosing me. Thank You for reminding me that I'm not just anybody—I'm part of Your royal priesthood. Help me to walk in this truth every day, no matter what the world says. I am Yours, and that's enough."

From that day on, Michelle's life began to change.

She started walking with a confidence she hadn't felt before. It wasn't arrogance—it was an assurance that came from knowing who she belonged to.

When she was overlooked or underestimated at work, she reminded herself, "I am chosen. I am royalty. I am God's special possession."

In her church, she began to speak up more, sharing her perspective and encouraging others with her testimony. She saw how her faith and her culture intertwined to create something beautiful—a reflection of God's creativity and love.

And when she mentored young Black girls in her community, she made it her mission to remind them of their worth. She would tell them, "You're not just anybody. You're part of a chosen generation. You're royalty. Don't ever forget that."

One afternoon, Michelle stood in front of a group of young girls at a community center and shared her story.

"I used to believe the lies the world told me—that I wasn't enough because of my skin, my gender, my faith. But then I found 1 Peter 2:9, and it changed everything. I realized that I'm not defined by what the world says about me. I'm defined by what God says about me. And He says I'm chosen, I'm royal, I'm loved."

The girls listened intently, their eyes wide.

"You don't have to shrink yourself to fit into a world that doesn't see your worth," Michelle continued. "You're already enough. You're already chosen. So, walk in that truth, and let God's light shine through you."

In the years that followed, Michelle's life became a testament to the power of God's Word. She faced challenges, but she faced them with the confidence of someone who knew she was deeply loved and divinely chosen.

Her faith and culture were no longer sources of tension—they were the foundation of her identity, woven together to create a powerful story of resilience and grace.

And every time she read 1 Peter 2:9, she smiled, knowing that she was walking in the marvelous light of the One who had called her out of darkness.

Prayer:

Lord, thank you for choosing me and calling me your own. Help me to live in a way that reflects your glory and to always remember my worth in you. Amen.

Affirmation: I am chosen, royal, and holy in God's sight.

Reflection Questions:

- Identity in Christ: How does 1 Peter 2:9 affirm your identity as a Black woman in Christ? In what ways can embracing this identity empower you to live out your faith boldly?
- Cultural Royalty: Reflect on the concept of being part of a "royal priesthood" and a "holy nation." How does this align with the artistic pride and heritage you hold as a Black woman?
- Called Out of Darkness: How has God called you out of darkness into His marvelous light in your personal life? How can this testimony impact other Black women who may feel overlooked or undervalued?
- Proclaiming God's Praises: How can you use your unique voice and experiences as a Black woman to declare the praises of God to those around you? What

are some specific ways you can do this in your community?

Notes:

DAY 24

Scripture: Galatians 6:9

"Let us not become weary in doing good, for at the proper time we will reap a harvest if we do not give up."

Devotional:

Danielle sat at her kitchen table, staring at the stack of bills in front of her. The small business she had poured her heart into—the community bookstore and café she had dreamed about for years—was barely staying afloat.

She opened Roots & Rhyme two years ago, determined to create a space where Black authors and artists could be celebrated, young kids could see themselves in the stories on the shelves, and the community could gather to dream and build together.

At first, the support had been overwhelming. The grand opening had been packed, with neighbors lining up to buy books and sip coffee. But as time went on, the excitement faded. Sales slowed, and the bills piled up.

Danielle felt like she was pushing a boulder uphill. She worked long hours, hosted events, and poured every ounce of her energy into the store, but it didn't seem to be enough.

Last night, she had cried herself to sleep, wondering if she had made a mistake. Maybe this dream wasn't meant to be. Perhaps she should give up.

As the morning light filtered through the window, Danielle reached for her Bible. She hadn't opened it in weeks—she had been so busy trying to fix everything on her own. But today, she felt an urge to turn to God.

Her fingers flipped to Galatians 6:9, a verse she had highlighted years ago:

"Let us not become weary in doing good, for at the proper time, we will reap a harvest if we do not give up."

Danielle reread the verse, tears welling up in her eyes.

"If we do not give up."

She let the words sink in. She had been so focused on what wasn't working that she had forgotten why she started this journey in the first place. She wasn't just running a business—she was planting seeds—seeds of representation, empowerment, and hope.

The harvest might not come overnight, but God had promised it would come.

Danielle whispered a prayer: "Lord, I'm tired. But I trust You. Help me to keep going, even when it's hard. I believe You'll bring the increase in Your time."

That afternoon, Danielle decided to take a step of faith. Instead of focusing on what wasn't working, she leaned into her purpose. She planned a community event—a storytelling night for kids featuring local Black authors. She reached out to her network, inviting schools, churches, and community groups.

The night of the event, Danielle felt a knot of nervousness in her stomach. What if no one showed up? What if this, too, was a failure?

But as the clock struck 6:00, families began to pour in. Parents and children filled the space, their laughter and chatter breathing life into the store. Local authors read stories that had the kids captivated, and the café buzzed with orders for hot chocolate and pastries.

Toward the end of the evening, one of the authors approached Danielle.

"Thank you for this," she said. "I've always dreamed of sharing my stories with kids who look like me. You've given us a platform, and that means everything."

Danielle felt a lump rise in her throat.

Later, as she looked around the room, she saw kids flipping through books, parents chatting with neighbors and smiles everywhere she turned. For the first time in a long time, she felt peace.

This wasn't just about sales or success—it was about impact. The seeds she was planting were taking root.

As the months went on, Danielle kept pressing forward. She continued to host events, collaborate with local artists, and find creative ways to serve her community.

It wasn't easy—there were still challenges and moments of doubt. But every time she felt like giving up, she remembered Galatians 6:9: "At the proper time, we will reap a harvest if we do not give up."

And slowly but surely, the harvest began to come.

A local newspaper featured Roots & Rhyme in an article about Black-owned businesses making a difference. Sales picked up as more people discovered the store. Grants and donations began to trickle in, allowing Danielle to expand her offerings.

One day, as she stood behind the counter, a young girl approached her with a book in hand.

"Miss Danielle," the girl said shyly, "I want to write books like this one day. Do you think I can?"

Danielle knelt to meet the girl's gaze. "I don't just think you can—I know you can. And when you do, this store will be the first to carry your books."

The girl beamed, and Danielle felt her heart swell

Looking back, Danielle realized that every challenge, every late night, every tear had been worth it. God had been faithful, just as He promised. The seeds she had planted were bearing fruit—not just in her business but in the lives of the people she served.

Danielle smiled as she flipped the sign on the door to "Open." She wasn't just running a bookstore. She was building a legacy. And she knew that, with God's help, the harvest would keep coming.

Prayer:

Lord, give me the strength to keep going, even when I feel like giving up. Remind me that my labor is not in vain and that you will bring a harvest in due season. Help me to persevere in doing good, trusting that you will reward my efforts.

Affirmation:

I will not grow weary in doing good, for in due season, I will reap a harvest if I do not give up.

Reflection Questions:

- As a Black woman, how do you maintain your strength and resilience when facing burnout while serving others in your family, church, or community? What specific challenges have you encountered in "doing good" without becoming weary?

- Throughout history, Black women have often been the backbone of their communities, persisting through adversity and injustice. How does this verse speak to your own experience of perseverance, and what "harvest" are you praying and working toward?
- Many Black women juggle multiple roles as caregivers, professionals, and community leaders. In what ways can you create healthy boundaries while still "doing good," and how do you discern when to rest versus when to persist?
- Reflect on the Black women in your life or history (like Harriet Tubman, Fannie Lou Hamer, or others) who demonstrated unwavering persistence in doing good. How does their example, combined with this scripture, inspire your journey of faith and service?

Notes:

DAY 25

Scripture: Psalm 30:2

"Lord my God, I called to you for help, and you healed me."

Devotional:

Amina stared at the ceiling of her bedroom, the soft hum of the fan barely masking the sound of her breathing. The world outside was asleep, but her mind refused to rest.

The diagnosis had come out of nowhere—a health challenge that left her feeling as though the ground beneath her had crumbled. She was used to being the strong one, the one people in her family and community leaned on. But now, as she lay there in the stillness of the night, it was her turn to feel weak, scared, and uncertain.

Amina's life had always been about others. She organized food drives, mentored young girls in her neighborhood, and cared for her aging parents. People often called her "the rock," a title she wore with pride. But tonight, the weight of being "the rock" felt unbearable.

She had been raised to be strong, to power through pain, to keep going no matter what. But this time, she couldn't.

As tears slid down her cheeks, Amina whispered into the darkness, "God, I don't know what to do. I need You. I can't do this on my own."

The admission felt foreign to her. She had always been the one offering prayers of gratitude, strength, and encouragement to others. Crying out for herself was new, but it was all she could do.

Her Bible sat on the nightstand, and she reached for it, flipping through the pages until her eyes landed on Psalm 30:2:

"O Lord my God, I cried to you for help, and you have healed me."

Amina reread the verse, her heart catching on the words. She closed the Bible and held it to her chest, letting the truth settle deep within her.

For so long, she had believed that strength meant carrying everything on her own. But here, in the quiet of her room, she realized that true strength came from surrender—laying her burdens at God's feet and trusting Him to carry her through.

"Lord," she prayed, her voice trembling, "I'm tired of trying to be strong on my own. I need Your strength. Heal me—not just my body, but my heart. Teach me to trust You completely."

In the days that followed, Amina began to approach her journey differently. She leaned into prayer, pouring out her fears, frustrations, and hopes to God. She shared her struggles with close friends and family, something she had never done before.

To her surprise, they rallied around her. Meals appeared at her doorstep. Her phone buzzed with texts of encouragement. Women from her church came to pray with her, their voices lifting her spirit even on her hardest days.

Amina began to see that she didn't have to be "the rock" all the time. She could lean on others, and more importantly, she could lean on God.

Psalm 30:2 became her anthem. Whenever doubt or fear crept in, she would whisper, *"O Lord my God, I cried to You for help, and You have healed me."*

Her healing wasn't instantaneous. It was a process—physical, emotional, and spiritual. But as she walked through it, Amina noticed something profound: her faith was deepening.

She began to see God's hand in the small things—a stranger's kind words at the doctor's office, a sunny day when she needed it most, a scripture verse showing up at just the right moment. These little reminders of God's love gave her the strength to keep going.

Months later, Amina stood in front of a group of women at her church, sharing her testimony.

"I used to think that being strong meant carrying everything on my own," she said, her voice steady. "But this journey has taught me that true strength comes from surrendering to God. When I cried out to Him, He didn't just heal my body—He healed my heart. He reminded me that I'm not alone and that His love is my ultimate source of strength."

The room was silent as Amina's words sank in.

"I know many of us were raised to believe we have to be strong all the time," she continued. "But let me tell you this: It's okay to need help. It's okay to cry out to God. He hears us. He loves us. And His strength is made perfect in our weakness."

After the gathering, a young woman approached Amina with tears in her eyes.

"Thank you for sharing," she said. "I've been trying to carry so much on my own, and I didn't realize how much it was weighing me down. Hearing your story gave me hope."

Amina smiled and hugged her, whispering, "You're not alone. God's got you."

As Amina walked to her car that evening, she looked up at the night sky. The stars seemed brighter; the air felt lighter.

She still had challenges to face, but she wasn't afraid. She knew now that her strength didn't come from herself—it came from the One who had carried her through.

"O Lord my God," she whispered, her heart full, "I cried to You for help, and You have healed me."

With that, Amina stepped into the next chapter of her life, more hopeful and confident than ever.

Prayer:

Lord, I come to you as your daughter, seeking your healing touch. Heal not just my body but my spirit and give me the strength to rely on you completely. In Jesus' name, Amen.

Affirmation:

I am healed and whole in God's love and grace. I trust in God's power to restore every part of me.

Reflection Questions:

- As a Black woman, in what ways have you experienced God's healing - whether physical, emotional, or spiritual - particularly in situations where traditional support systems or healthcare may have failed you? How has this shaped your faith?
- Black women often carry heavy burdens silently while caring for others. When was a time you

allowed yourself to be vulnerable and "called out" to God for help? What made it difficult or easy to do so?
- Given the historical and ongoing health disparities affecting Black women, how does this verse strengthen your faith in God as the ultimate healer? How can it empower you to advocate for both spiritual and physical wellness in your community?
- Reflect on the healing traditions and faith practices passed down through generations of Black women in your family or community. How do these traditions, combined with this scripture, inform your understanding of God's healing power today?

Notes:

DAY 26

Scripture: 2 Corinthians 12:9

"My grace is sufficient for you, for my power is made perfect in weakness."

Devotional:

Andrea didn't know what it meant to take a break. For as long as she could remember, she was the one everyone relied on. She worked full-time at a demanding job, cared for her aging mother, and was the unofficial problem-solver for her siblings and friends. Andrea was there if someone needed help moving. If someone needed a ride to the airport, Andrea was driving. She never said no because she thought that's what love looked like: showing up, no matter how tired she was.

But lately, the cracks were starting to show. She was snapping at her coworkers over little things, forgetting appointments, and waking up at 3 a.m. with her mind racing. Even her body was starting to rebel—her back ached constantly, and her energy was nonexistent. Andrea told herself she was fine—it was just stress—but one night, after a tough day, she couldn't hold it together anymore.

She got home, parked in her driveway, and just sat there. The silence in her car felt deafening. Before she knew it, tears were streaming down her face. She cried until she couldn't cry anymore. Through her tears, she whispered, "God, I'm so tired. I can't do this anymore. I don't have anything left to give."

Andrea didn't expect anything to happen. She felt empty, broken, and hopeless. But in that quiet moment, she felt something shift. It wasn't a loud voice or a miraculous sign—

it was just a thought that floated into her mind as clear as day: *"You don't have to."*

Those words stayed with her as she went to bed that night. The following morning, Andrea woke up with a scripture on her heart: *"My grace is sufficient for you, for my power is made perfect in weakness."* The words echoed in her mind all day. It was like God was reminding her that she didn't have to carry everything on her own. His grace was enough.

That day, Andrea made a choice. She started small. She began praying in the mornings, asking God to show her what was hers to carry and what she needed to let go of. For the first time in years, she said no when a friend asked for a favor she couldn't handle. It was hard at first—she felt guilty—but she reminded herself that her worth wasn't tied to how much she could do for others.

She also started saying yes to things that brought her peace and joy. She went on a walk during her lunch break instead of working through it. She sat down with her mother and enjoyed her company instead of rushing around doing chores. And when a coworker offered to help with a project, Andrea surprised herself by saying yes.

At first, the changes felt strange, almost uncomfortable. But over time, Andrea began to feel lighter—not because her responsibilities disappeared, but because she stopped trying to carry them all by herself. She let God step in and carry the weight with her.

Today, Andrea's life isn't perfect, but it's different. She's learned that being strong doesn't mean doing everything on her own. It means trusting God to give her the grace to do what really matters. And that's more than enough.

Prayer:

God, teach me to wait on you with a heart full of hope. Let me trust in Your timing, knowing that Your plans for me are good. In Jesus' name, Amen.

Affirmation:

I am patient, trusting in God's perfect timing for my life.

Reflection Questions:

- How might viewing God's grace as "sufficient" change the way you approach your challenges?
- What parts of your story show how God's strength carried you when you couldn't carry yourself? How can you share that testimony with others?
- What burdens are you carrying right now that you need to surrender to God?
- How can you intentionally practice trusting God's grace in those areas this week?

Notes:

DAY 27

Scripture: Psalm 46:5

"God is within her; she will not fall; God will help her at break of day."

Devotional:

Janelle stared at the acceptance letter on her kitchen table for the tenth time that morning. She had done it—she had applied to the community college she'd been eyeing for years, and they had accepted her. But instead of feeling proud or excited, she felt paralyzed with fear.

She was a 39-year-old single mom, and the thought of going back to school after all these years terrified her. "What if I fail?" she thought. "What if I'm too old? What if I can't keep up with the younger students? What if I disappoint my kids?"

Janelle had always dreamed of becoming a nurse, but life had gotten in the way. First, she was taking care of her siblings after her mom passed. Then, it was working two jobs to support her kids. Now, after years of putting everyone else first, she finally had a chance to focus on herself—but the fear of failing was so loud it almost drowned out the hope.

One Sunday morning, Janelle sat in church, trying to hold back tears. During the sermon, the pastor quoted Psalm 46:5: *"God is within her, she will not fall; God will help her at break of day."* The words hit her like a wave. She scribbled them down in her notebook and looked at them over and over again.

That night, as she lay in bed, she whispered a prayer: "God, I'm scared. I don't know if I can do this. But if You're with me, help me believe that I won't fail. Help me take the first step."

The following day, Janelle woke up early and sat at the kitchen table with her acceptance letter again. This time, instead of focusing on her fears, she focused on God's promise. She told herself, "If God is with me, I don't have to have it all figured out. I have to trust Him with the next step."

Over the next few weeks, Janelle prepared for her first semester. She bought her books, signed up for her classes, and even joined a study group for adult learners. Each step felt like a leap of faith, but she kept reminding herself of Psalm 46:5: *"God is within her; she will not fall."*

When the first day of class came, Janelle was nervous, but she showed up anyway. She smiled at her classmates, introduced herself to her professor, and took her seat in the front row. As the class began, she felt a sense of peace wash over her. She realized that she wasn't doing this alone—God was with her every step of the way.

Now, months into her program, Janelle looks back on that acceptance letter and smiles. She's thriving in her classes, her kids are proud of her, and she's one step closer to her dream of becoming a nurse. Whenever fear tries to creep back in, she reminds herself of God's promise: "I will not fall because God is within me."

Prayer:

God, Thank you for reminding me that you are within me and that I will not fall. When fear and doubt creep in, help me to trust in your strength and guidance. Give me the courage to take each step, knowing that you will help me, even at the break of the day. I surrender my fears to you and ask for your peace to fill my heart. Thank you for being my constant source of strength and for walking this journey with me.

Affirmation:

God is within me, and I will not fall. I am strong, capable, and supported by God's unfailing help every step of the way."

Reflection Questions:

- What does it mean to you that "God is within her"? Reflect on how God's presence in your life provides strength and confidence. How does this truth change the way you face challenges?
- When have you experienced God helping you "at the break of day"? Think about a time when God showed up for you in a moment of need. How did His presence give you the strength to keep moving forward?
- What fears or doubts are you currently facing? Identify the areas in your life where you feel uncertain or weak. How can you remind yourself of Psalm 46:5 when those fears arise?
- How can you encourage yourself and others with this scripture? Who in your life might need to hear this promise of God's presence and strength? How can you use this verse to uplift them or yourself in difficult times?

Notes:

DAY 28

Scripture: Psalm 51: 1-2

"Have mercy on me, O God,

according to your unfailing love;

according to your great compassion

blot out my transgressions.

2 Wash away all my iniquity

and cleanse me from my sin."

Devotional:

Tamika had always been the rock for everyone else. As the oldest sibling in her family and the trusted friend in her circle, people counted on her for advice, support, and guidance. She prided herself on being dependable and wise, the one who always seemed to have it together. But when Tamika made a choice, she deeply regretted—a choice that went against her values—everything she thought she knew about herself crumbled.

The guilt was unbearable. She replayed her mistake over and over in her mind, each time feeling more ashamed. "How could I let this happen?" she thought. What if people find out? What if God gives up on me?" Tamika tried to brush it off and keep moving forward as if nothing had happened, but the weight of her sin stayed with her. It seeped into her thoughts, prayers, and relationships.

Growing up, Tamika was taught to be strong, never show weakness, and never let anyone see her struggle. So, instead of sharing her pain, she buried it deep inside. But the more she tried to ignore it, the more it consumed her. She began to feel like she wasn't worthy of love—not from others, and especially not from God.

One quiet evening, in the midst of her despair, Tamika picked up her Bible and turned to the Psalms. Her eyes fell on Psalm 51. As she read David's words, her heart softened:

"Have mercy on me, O God, according to your unfailing love; according to your great compassion, blot out my transgressions. Wash away all my iniquity and cleanse me from my sin."

The words felt like they were written just for her. For the first time in weeks, Tamika allowed herself to feel the full weight of her emotions—not just the guilt but also the deep longing for God's forgiveness and mercy.

Through her tears, she whispered a prayer: "God, I've messed up. I don't even know where to begin, but I need Your mercy. Please, wash me clean. Help me believe that You still love me, even after all I've done."

That night, something began to shift in Tamika. She realized that asking for forgiveness wasn't just about clearing her record with God—it was about letting go of the shame that had been holding her captive. She began to see that God's love wasn't conditional; it wasn't based on her ability always to get it right. His passion was unfailing, and His mercy was more significant than her mistakes.

Over the next few weeks, Tamika started practicing something that felt foreign to her: self-compassion. She reminded herself that she was human, that everyone fell short, and that God's grace was big enough to cover her failures. She wrote Psalm 51:1–2 on a sticky note and placed it on her bathroom mirror. Every morning, as she got ready for the day, she read those words and reminded herself that she was forgiven and deeply loved.

Tamika also began journaling to process her feelings. She wrote about her guilt, her fears, and, most importantly, her hope. She stopped trying to be perfect and started focusing on being honest—with God, with herself, and with the people she trusted.

One day, as she was journaling, God whispered to her heart, *"You are not defined by your mistakes. You are defined by My love."* Those words became her anchor.

Tamika's journey wasn't easy. There were still moments when the shame tried to creep back in, but each time it did, she fought back with God's truth. She reminded herself that she was forgiven, loved, and made new. She leaned into God's unfailing love and allowed His mercy to heal her heart.

Looking back, Tamika sees her mistake not as the end of her story but as a turning point. It was the moment she realized that God's grace is bigger than any failure and that forgiveness isn't just something to receive—it's something to embrace.

Today, Tamika uses her story to encourage others who feel weighed down by guilt and shame. "God's mercy is real," she says. "It's not just for the people who seem to have it all together—it's for all of us, especially when we feel broken. You're never too far gone for God's love."

Tamika's journey reminds us that God's compassion and forgiveness are always available, no matter how far we fall. He doesn't just cleanse us from our sins—He restores us, renews us, and teaches us how to love ourselves the way He loves us.

Prayer:

Merciful God, I come to you with a repentant heart. Cleanse me from my sins and restore me to the joy of your salvation. In Jesus' name, Amen.

Affirmation:

I am forgiven and cleansed by God's unfailing love and mercy.

Reflection Questions:

- As a Black woman, society often holds you to impossible standards of being "strong" or "perfect." How does this psalm's message of seeking God's mercy and compassion help you embrace vulnerability and release the pressure of these expectations? When was the last time you allowed yourself to simply rest in God's compassion?
- The phrase "unfailing love" speaks to God's consistent, unconditional love. In a world that often devalues or misunderstands Black women, how does knowing God's love is unfailing impact your sense of worth and identity? How has experiencing God's unfailing love helped heal from experiences where human love has failed?
- David speaks of being "cleansed" and "washed." For Black women who have experienced trauma, discrimination, or carried others' burdens, what areas of their lives need God's deep cleansing? How can embracing God's forgiveness help them extend forgiveness to themselves?
- Many Black women carry generational pain or patterns that need healing. How does this psalm's promise of complete cleansing speak to both personal

and generational healing? What would it look like to fully receive God's mercy in these areas?

Notes:

DAY 29

Scripture: Ephesians 2:10

"For we are God's handiwork, created in Christ Jesus to do good works, which God prepared in advance for us to do."

Devotional:

Nia had always felt the weight of expectation. The unspoken rules of her upbringing were clear: As a young Black woman, she had to work twice as hard, be twice as perfect, and achieve twice as much just to be seen, respected, or heard. She carried this mindset into every area of her life—from school to her career, even into her relationships.

On the outside, Nia looked like she had it all together. She graduated at the top of her class, landed a prestigious job, and was the friend everyone admired. But on the inside, she felt exhausted and empty. No matter how much she accomplished, it never felt like enough. She was always chasing the next goal, the next accolade, the subsequent validation, hoping it would finally make her feel worthy.

One evening, after an especially grueling week at work, Nia sat in her apartment, drained. She had poured her heart into a project only to have her boss criticize it. Her mind raced with questions: "What did I do wrong? Why wasn't it good enough? Why am I not good enough?"

Out of habit, she opened her Bible app, not expecting much. The verse of the day was Ephesians 2:10: *"For we are God's handiwork, created in Christ Jesus to do good works, which God prepared in advance for us to do."*

The words stopped her in her tracks. She reread them, slower this time. *God's handiwork.* Nia let that sink in. Could it really be true? Could she really be God's masterpiece—not because of what she did, but because of who He created her to be?

For years, Nia had tied her worth to her performance, but this verse told a different story. It said her value came from God, the Creator of the universe, who had designed her with care and intention. Suddenly, she realized that her achievements didn't define her; God did.

That night, Nia prayed a simple prayer: "God, help me to see myself the way You see me. Teach me to rest in the truth that I am Your masterpiece."

As the days passed, Nia began to meditate on Ephesians 2:10. She wrote it on a sticky note and placed it on her bathroom mirror. Every morning, as she got ready for work, she repeated the words to herself: *"I am God's handiwork. I am created with a purpose. I am enough."*

This truth didn't change her circumstances overnight, but it changed her heart. She started to notice how often she pushed herself to prove her worth, and she began to challenge those thoughts. When she felt the urge to overwork herself, she paused and reminded herself that her value wasn't tied to her productivity.

One day, during a team meeting, Nia spoke up and shared an idea she had been sitting on for weeks. In the past, she would have second-guessed herself, worried that her idea wasn't perfect. But this time, she spoke confidently, knowing that her worth wasn't on the line. Her idea was well-received, and for the first time, she felt free—not because of the praise, but because she no longer needed it to feel good about herself.

As Nia leaned into her identity as God's masterpiece, she also began to see her purpose more clearly. She realized that the gifts and passions God had given her weren't about proving her value—they were about glorifying Him and serving others. She started volunteering at a local mentorship program for young girls, sharing her story and encouraging them to embrace their worth in Christ.

Through it all, Nia learned to rest in the fact that God had already prepared good works for her to do. She didn't have to strive or compete for her place in the world—God already set her purpose.

Today, Nia walks with a confidence that comes not from her achievements but from her identity in Christ. She still works hard and pursues excellence, but she does so from a place of freedom, not pressure. She knows she is loved, valued, and enough—not because of what she does but because of who she is: God's handiwork.

Whenever she feels old doubts creeping in, she recalls Ephesians 2:10 and reminds herself: *"I am God's masterpiece, created in Christ Jesus to do good works. My worth is secure in Him."*

Nia's story is a testament to the transformative power of understanding our identity in Christ. It reminds us that we don't have to hustle for our worth—it's already been given to us by the One who created us with love and purpose.

Prayer:

God, help me to see myself as your masterpiece, created for good works that you have already prepared for me. Let me walk in my purpose with confidence and grace. In Jesus' name, Amen.

Affirmation:

I am God's masterpiece, created for a purpose, and I walk confidently in the good works God has prepared for me.

Reflection Questions:

- As a Black woman, how does knowing you are God's "handiwork" (God's) masterpiece) challenge or heal any negative messages you've received about your worth, beauty, or capabilities - whether from society, media, or personal experiences? How does this truth specifically affirm your identity as a Black woman?
- Throughout history, Black women have often been defined by what they do (caregiving, serving, working) rather than who they are. How does this verse's order - being God's handiwork first, then doing good works - reshape your understanding of your value and purpose? How can you maintain this identity-first perspective in your daily life?
- The verse speaks of works "prepared in advance." Reflecting on the legacy of Black women who came before you (in your family, church, or community), how do you see God's preparation at work in your own life? What unique gifts, experiences, or perspectives has He given you to fulfill your purpose?
- God's advanced preparation suggests intentionality and purpose. As a Black woman navigating various spaces (professional, personal, spiritual), how does knowing God has specifically prepared works for you empower you to walk confidently in your calling, even in environments where you might be the only one? What "good works" do you believe God has uniquely positioned you to do?

Notes:

DAY 30

Scripture: Matthew 11:28

"Come to me, all you who are weary and burdened, and I will give you rest."

Devotional:

Mariah was the definition of a strong Black woman. She was a wife, a mother, a daughter, a sister, a mentor, and a leader in her community. She wore her strength like a badge of honor—never letting anyone see her sweat, never asking for help, and always showing up for everyone else.

Her days started before the sun rose and ended long after it set. She packed lunches, led meetings, volunteered at church, helped her aging parents, and stayed up late to finish work that spilled over into her evenings. People admired her, calling her "superwoman," and she smiled and accepted the praise. But deep down, Mariah felt like she was drowning.

No one saw the tears she cried in the shower or the anxiety that gripped her chest as she juggled the never-ending demands of life. No one saw how exhausted she felt—physically, emotionally, and spiritually. She had convinced herself that rest was a luxury she couldn't afford. After all, who else would hold everything together if she stopped?

One Sunday morning, Mariah sat in church, barely listening to the sermon. Her mind was racing with her to-do list for the week. But then the pastor read Matthew 11:28: *"Come to me, all you who are weary and burdened, and I will give you rest."*

The words pierced through her exhaustion: rest. It was such a simple word, but it felt so far out of reach. She couldn't remember the last time she truly rested—not just physically but mentally and spiritually. The pastor continued, "Jesus is inviting you to lay your burdens down. You don't have to carry them alone. He wants to give you His peace, His rest."

Mariah felt tears welling up in her eyes. She had been carrying so much for so long, and she didn't even realize how heavy it had become. She whispered a silent prayer: "Lord, I'm so tired. I don't know how to let go, but I need Your rest. Please help me."

That afternoon, Mariah sat on her porch with her Bible and a journal. She reread Matthew 11:28 slowly this time. She wrote down everything that had been weighing on her heart: the pressure to be perfect, the fear of letting others down, the guilt of saying no, and the overwhelming fatigue that never seemed to go away.

As she wrote, God whispered to her heart, *"You don't have to do it all. I didn't create you to carry every burden on your own. Come to Me. Let Me carry this with you."*

For the first time in years, Mariah allowed herself to release the weight she had been carrying. She cried, not out of despair, but out of relief. She realized that being strong didn't mean doing everything alone—it meant trusting God with the things she couldn't handle.

Over the next few weeks, Mariah began making small but meaningful changes. She started each day with prayer, asking God to guide her steps and give her wisdom. She learned to say no to commitments that drained her energy. She asked her husband and children for help around the house, realizing she didn't have to do everything herself.

Mariah also made time for rest—not just sleep, but true rest. She spent time in God's presence, reading His Word and worshiping without an agenda. She took walks in the park, enjoying the beauty of creation. She reconnected with friends who refreshed her soul.

As she surrendered her burdens to God, Mariah began to feel lighter. The anxiety that once consumed her started to fade, replaced by a deep sense of peace. She was still busy—life didn't stop—but she no longer felt the need to prove her worth by how much she accomplished.

Mariah realized that her value didn't come from being strong all the time. Her strength came from God, who was inviting her to rest in Him. She didn't have to be superwoman—she just had to be obedient to the One who loved her and called her His own.

Today, Mariah is still the strong Black woman everyone admires, but her strength looks different now. It's not the kind of strength that comes from overworking herself or carrying every burden alone. It's the kind of strength that comes from trusting God with her life, her family, her work, and her rest.

When people ask her how she does it all, she smiles and says, "I don't. I've learned to give it to God and let Him carry me. His rest is my strength."

Mariah's story reminds us that we don't have to wear ourselves out to prove our worth. Jesus invites us to come to Him, to lay down our burdens, and to find rest in His presence. When we do, we discover that true strength isn't about doing it all—it's about trusting the One who already has it all under control.

Prayer:

Lord, thank you for inviting me to come to you when I'm weary and burdened. I surrender all my stress, worries, and responsibilities to you today. Teach me to rest in your presence and trust that you are in control. Fill me with your peace and renew my strength as I lean on you. Thank you for being my refuge and my rest. In Jesus' name, Amen.

Affirmation:

I am not alone in my burdens. I am invited to rest in God's presence, where I find peace, strength, and renewal.

Reflection Questions:

- What burdens are you currently carrying, and how can you bring them to God? Reflect on the areas of your life where you feel overwhelmed. How does Jesus' invitation to rest give you hope?
- What does it mean to you to "come to Jesus"? Consider the practical ways you can draw closer to Him when you're feeling weary or burdened.
- Why do you think it's often hard for people to rest or ask for help? Explore the cultural or personal reasons that make it difficult to release control and trust God with your struggles.
- How does trusting God with your burdens change the way you view yourself and your circumstances? Think about how surrendering to God can bring peace and strength, even in challenging situations.

Notes:

DAY 31

Scripture: Joshua 24:15

"But if serving the Lord seems undesirable to you, then choose for yourselves this day whom you will serve, whether the gods your ancestors served beyond the Euphrates or the gods of the Amorites, in whose land you are living. But as for me and my household, we will serve the Lord."

Devotional:

Egypt sat alone in her car, staring at the steering wheel. The parking lot was empty, and the hum of streetlights was the only sound breaking the silence of the night. She had just come from another long day at work, and her mind was racing. On the surface, she had everything she thought she wanted—a corporate job in a downtown high-rise, a luxury apartment, and the kind of clothes that made people notice when she walked into a room.

But deep down, Egypt felt hollow, empty. Something was missing.

She had grown up in church, sitting next to her grandmother every Sunday morning in the second pew. Her grandmother's faith was unshakable, and she often told Egypt, "Baby, no matter what life throws at you, always choose God." Egypt would nod obediently, but as she got older, her life began to pull her in a different direction.

In college, she chose to chase success. She threw herself into internships, networking events, and late-night study sessions, leaving little room for prayer, church, or even quiet moments with God. After graduation, her career became her focus. She told herself there would be time for God later—after the next promotion, after the next significant milestone.

But now, sitting in her car, Egypt couldn't ignore the truth anymore. She was tired—tired of pretending everything was fine, tired of chasing things that never seemed to satisfy her, and tired of feeling so far from the God she once knew so well.

Her phone buzzed, snapping her out of her thoughts. It was a text from her best friend, Simone, who had been inviting her to a Bible study for months.

"Hey, sis! Just checking on you. Bible study is tomorrow night. No pressure, but you're always welcome!"

Egypt sighed. Simone had been so patient with her. She had declined every invitation, always claiming she was too busy. But tonight, looking at the text, she felt something stir in her. Maybe it was her grandmother's voice echoing in her heart: *"Always choose God."*

She glanced at the small Bible in her glove compartment. It had been a gift from her grandmother, though it had gone unopened for far too long. She pulled it out and flipped through its pages, landing on Joshua 24:15:

"But if serving the LORD seems undesirable to you, then choose for yourselves this day whom you will serve...but as for me and my household, we will serve the LORD."

The words hit her like a bolt of lightning. Choose. She had been making choices her whole life—choices about her career, her relationships, her priorities—but she had been avoiding the most important one. Who would she serve?

Egypt closed her eyes and whispered a prayer, the first one she had said in months. "God, I don't know what I'm doing. I've been running for so long, chasing things that don't matter. But I'm tired, and I'm ready to come back to You.

Help me choose You. Help me let go of everything that's been keeping me from You."

The next evening, Egypt walked into Simone's Bible study with her heart pounding. She felt out of place at first, but as the group began to read and discuss the Word, something inside her softened. For the first time in years, she felt a sense of peace—a sense of home.

Choosing God didn't make her life instantly perfect. There were still challenges at work, still moments of doubt and struggle. But now, Egypt had something she hadn't felt in a long time: hope. She began to pray daily, read her Bible, and attend church regularly. She even started sharing her faith with her coworkers, finding ways to let her light shine in the corporate world.

One Sunday morning, as she sat in the second pew of her church, Egypt thought of her grandmother. She could almost hear her voice, filled with pride and joy: *"Baby, you made the right choice. Always choose God."*

Egypt smiled; her heart full. She knew that choosing God wasn't just a one-time decision—it was a daily commitment. But she was ready to make it every single day.

Prayer:

Lord, help me to stand firm in my faith and to lead my family in a way that honors you. May our home be a place where your name is always lifted high. Amen.

Affirmation:

My household serves the Lord, and God's word guides our steps.

Reflection Questions:

- Joshua 24:15 speaks about making a conscious choice to serve the Lord. How does this verse challenge you to establish a legacy of faith within your family, especially considering the cultural heritage of Black women?
- How does your cultural identity influence your decision to serve the Lord? In what ways can this decision impact the broader community of Black women?
- What are some modern-day idols or distractions that challenge your commitment to serving God? How can you reaffirm your choice to prioritize your faith in your daily life?
- As a Black woman, how can you lead by example in your household and community, showing others what it means to choose to serve the Lord?

Notes:

Epilogue

To my beautiful Black sisters,

As we reach the end of this 31-day journey together, I want to take a moment to speak directly to your heart.

You are *loved*. Deeply. Fiercely. Eternally. Not just for what you do, how you show up for others, or the strength you carry so effortlessly on your shoulders. You are loved simply because you exist because God created you, in all your brilliance and beauty, as a reflection of God's glory.

I see you. I know the weight you carry—the responsibilities you hold, the silent battles you fight, the dreams you've put on hold to care for others. I see the tears you cry in private and the resilience you display in public. I know the strength you've had to summon in a world that often doesn't see you clearly. But even more importantly, God sees you. God sees every part of you, even the parts you think aren't worthy of love. God sees the little girl who first dreamed of what her life could be. God sees the woman you are now, navigating life with grace, faith, and perseverance. God sees the woman you are becoming—the one who is learning to trust God more fully, rest in God's promises and embrace the fullness of who God created you to be.

Sister, you are not forgotten. You are not invisible. You are not merely strong—you are sacred. You are a masterpiece, woven together by the hands of a loving Creator who calls you His own.

This devotional was written as a love offering to you, a reminder that you are not alone in this journey. You are part of a sisterhood that spans generations—a lineage of women who have prayed, praised, and persevered through everything life has thrown at them. And just as God carried them, He will carry you.

I pray that over these 31 days, you've felt God's presence, God's peace, and God's power in your life. I pray that you've been reminded of your worth, your purpose, and the unshakable truth that you are God's beloved.

As you move forward, I want you to remember this: You don't have to have it all figured out, and you don't have to be perfect. God's grace is sufficient for you, and God's strength is made perfect in your weakness. Let go of the pressures, the expectations, and the lies that say you're not enough. You are more than enough because you are God's.

Take these words with you: You are a queen. You are a warrior. You are a woman of faith, power, and purpose. And no matter what life brings, you will rise because the One who conquered the grave lives inside of you. So, my sister, keep shining, keep growing, and keep loving yourself as deeply as God loves you. And always remember: You are seen, valued, and loved.

With all my heart,

Dr. Tasha

www.ingramcontent.com/pod-product-compliance
Lightning Source LLC
Chambersburg PA
CBHW070734230426
43665CB00016B/2236